Finding Your Bearings

Finding Your Bearings

*How Words That Guided Jesus through Crisis
Can Guide Us*

James A. Harnish

FOREWORD BY
Paul W. Chilcote

CASCADE *Books* • Eugene, Oregon

FINDING YOUR BEARINGS
How Words That Guided Jesus Through Crisis Can Guide Us

Cascade Books
An Imprint of Wipf and Stock Publishers
199 W. 8th Ave., Suite 3
Eugene, OR 97401

www.wipfandstock.com

PAPERBACK ISBN: 978-1-7252-9588-9
HARDCOVER ISBN: 978-1-7252-9587-2
EBOOK ISBN: 978-1-7252-9589-6

Cataloguing-in-Publication data:

Names: Harnish, James A., author. | Chilcote, Paul Wesley, 1954–, foreword.

Title: Finding your bearings : how words that guided Jesus through crisis can guide us / by James A. Harnish ; foreword by Paul W. Chilcote.

Description: Eugene, OR : Cascade Books, 2021 | Includes bibliographical references.

Identifiers: ISBN 978-1-7252-9588-9 (paperback) | ISBN 978-1-7252-9587-2 (hardcover) | ISBN 978-1-7252-9589-6 (ebook)

Subjects: LCSH: Spiritual life—Christianity.

Classification: BV4501.3 .H38 2021 (print) | BV4501.3 .H38 (ebook)

07/16/21

With Gratitude for Jack,
brother in the womb, brother in ministry,
and brother on the way.

In this process of Christian growing up, one of the most difficult things is the sense we will have that we have lost our bearings on the way . . . When the signposts and landmarks have been taken away there is a presence that does not let you go. And that is faith.

—Rowan Williams, 104th Archbishop of Canterbury[1]

1. Williams, *Being Disciples*, 21, 25.

Contents

Foreword

As I have observed my friend Jim Harnish over the years, he always seems to be driven by one overriding question: "How can I help people grow more fully in their faith and into the loving people God would have them to be?" That question comes from the depths of a pastor's heart. Jim takes "the care of souls" seriously. His assumption is that if disciples of Jesus are serious about their relationship with God, they will want to grow in their faith. Over the years he has produced a wide range of resources for God's people, both laity and clergy, to engage the Word of God, explore more fully their own personal faith, examine their deepest questions, and he has always encouraged them to do this in community.

Jim first mentioned the idea he had for this book at the close of a lovely dinner we shared together with our spouses as we walked out to our cars in the parking lot. Like many parking-lot conversations, it triggered so many thoughts and subsequent reflections. My initial reaction was to say, "I can't think of any book I've read that does what you hope to do in this one." I was not surprised, because this is simply a factor of Jim's creative mind. Months later, when I had my first opportunity to review his manuscript, I was so pleased primarily because of the interface of his original idea with the particular times in which we are living today. I cannot think of a more critical time in which we need good guidance on finding our bearings!

As you prepare to launch into this adventurous journey, remember these salient characteristics about the shepherd guiding you through this study. First, for Jim, the beginning point, ending point, and the journey itself are all about Jesus. Take your bearings from the "pioneer and perfecter of our faith" (Heb 12:2). Second, for Jim, the whole Bible matters. The insights you will encounter here with regard to how Jesus used the Hebrew Scriptures so as to bring them to life will amaze you. Open your heart to the whole Word of God. Third, for Jim, the questions are often more important than the answers. He has done a phenomenal job of laying important questions before you. Engage them fully, and all the better if you hash out your responses in the context of a small group. Finally, for Jim, life is filled with hope and love. So, in the pages that follow, seek it out. Keep not only yours eyes but your heart open to the glimmers of hope and the signposts of love. They will be surrounding you at virtually every point in the journey as you find your bearings.

Paul W. Chilcote

Methodist theologian and award-winning author

Orientation

B ad things can happen if we lose our bearings.

January 26, 2020, 9:06 a.m., Pacific Standard Time. A Sikorsky helicopter took off from John Wayne Airport in Orange County, California, with nine passengers including Lakers's star basketball player, Kobe Bryant, his thirteen-year-old daughter, Gianna, and six family friends. They were on their way to a basketball game in Thousand Oaks.

At 9:30 a.m., the pilot notified the tower they were experiencing extremely heavy fog. At 9:45 a.m., the helicopter crashed into the side of a mountain about thirty miles northwest of downtown Los Angeles. The pilot and all the passengers were killed. News reports said the pilot was disoriented by the weather conditions, telling air traffic controllers that he was climbing when he was actually descending.

The tragedy sent shock waves across the nation in the early weeks of a year that would contain more than its full share of disorienting crises. It was a heart-wrenching reminder that there are potentially disastrous consequences if we lose our bearings.

By contrast, retired four-star Admiral James Stavridis, the former Supreme Allied Commander of NATO, recounted the ways some of history's greatest naval heroes found their bearings in his book, *Sailing True North: Ten Admirals and the Voyage of Character*. He acknowledged, "The challenges I wrestled with most frequently were inside, as I sought to set my own compass to True North."[1]

In navigation, "bearing" determines a ship's location in relation to True North. "Finding our bearings" is the way we locate where we are and set our course to get to where we want to be. It's also a practical metaphor for the way we determine the orientation of our lives and make decisions about the way we will follow to reach our goal or destination.

German theologian Jürgen Moltmann used the same metaphor when he described followers of Christ as "men and women who are on the way in the conflict of history and are *looking for bearings on that way*."[2] Following Jesus means finding our bearings through the crises, conflicts, and confusion of our lives by walking the way Jesus walked in the way that Jesus walked it. Eugene Peterson underscored the double meaning of the noun *way* to describe "not only the way we go, as in the route we take, but the way we go on the way."[3]

How Jesus Found His Bearings

I was exploring the places in the gospels where Jesus specifically quoted the Old Testament when I discovered that many of them are at crucial turning points in his life or the lives of his followers. In those crisis moments, Jesus found his bearings in the words and stories he inherited from the Hebrew scriptures, also called the Old Testament. That's when I ran head-on into a fact that is as obvious as it is easily missed: Jesus was a Jew.

Like Tevye in the Broadway musical *Fiddler on the Roof* Jesus' worldview was formed within a tradition centered around a passionate devotion to and a life-shaping love for the Hebrew Scriptures. He grew up in a home where his parents practiced the Levitical law. His understanding of God was formed in the

---

1. Stavridis, *Sailing True North*, xviii.

2. Moltmann, *Way of Jesus*, xiii. Emphasis mine.

3. Peterson, *Jesus Way*, 22.

synagogue where he regularly heard the Scripture read and listened as it was vigorously debated.

The things Jesus taught and the way Jesus lived confirm that during his developmental years that are hidden in silence, words from the Hebrew Scriptures were imbedded so deeply in his mind and soul that they became the internal GPS that kept him on course when he might have been diverted to go in a different way. Words from the only Scriptures he knew became compass points that kept him moving toward the True North of God's calling in his life.

This is your invitation to walk with me into six crucial moments in the Gospels when Jesus found his bearings by recalling words and stories from the Hebrew Scriptures. We'll enter into the settings in which Jesus recalled words and stories that emerged spontaneously in each crisis in his life or the lives of his followers. We'll explore the context in which these ancient words were first spoken. We'll hear the biblical texts through the voices of Christian tradition, in our shared experience in the community of faith, and with the presence of the Holy Spirit, who Jesus promised would "remind us of all that [he] said" (John 14:26). Along the way, we'll find our bearings for our own lives as we walk the way that Jesus walked in the way that Jesus walked it.

The Annus Horribilis

Books are written in a specific moment in time with the hope that they speak to timeless realities. This book came to life during the converging crises of 2020. The odds are that we look back on that year the way Queen Elizabeth declared 1992 to be an *Annus Horribilis*. Along with crises in her nation and around the world, the fortieth year of her reign was also the year three of her children's marriages ended in divorce and Windsor Castle burned. She confessed with unaccustomed candor that it was "not a year on which I shall look back with undiluted pleasure." She went on to say, "There are very few people or institutions unaffected by these last months of worldwide turmoil and uncertainty."[4]

4. Elizabeth, "Annus Horribilis Speech."

In 2020, the global coronavirus pandemic, its disastrous impact on the economy, our national reckoning with systemic racism, and a divisive presidential election unearthed sinister realities that lurked beneath the highly polished veneer of what we thought of as success and social progress. We also confronted the crisis of climate change with raging fires in the West and devastating hurricanes in the South. Houses, street signs, and landmarks were wiped away so that people had a hard time finding their bearings in formerly familiar places.

The crises of our *Annus Horribilis* were different only in degree of magnitude from the low magnitude crises that never appear as breaking news on the cable news networks, but which disrupt our comfortable lives with disturbing regularity. These crises, in whatever form they come, push open doors to hidden chambers in our souls, often exposing the hollowness of our biblical and spiritual resources. They lay bare our need for an internal compass that will guide us through the extraordinary challenges of our ordinary lives.

"But wait!"—as they shout on the TV infomercials—"There's more!"

Queen Elizabeth kept calm and carried on! She found her bearings through the *Annus Horribilis* and was very much alive in the sixty-eighth year of her reign, offering an example of stability and hope for all of us. As people of biblical faith, we can find personal stability and unswerving hope in the assurance that the God who walked with people through crises in the past is still at work in every crisis to fulfill the redeeming, life-giving purpose that became flesh among us in Jesus Christ.

Finding Our Bearings

My study of the way Jesus found his bearings at crucial points in the Gospels led to renewing convictions about how we can find our way through the crises of our lives, whatever form they take and whenever they come.

A crisis is a terrible thing to waste.

Every crisis is an opportunity to dig deeper and stretch farther. Crises can lure us back into cozy myths and convenient assumptions of an often mythical past or they can urge us along the way that leads to a new and more challenging future. Every crisis creates the opportunity to make long-overdue changes in the way we think, act, and live as followers of Christ. We do not "return to normal" after a crisis but find our way into a "new normal" that has been forged in the crucible of human experience.

Every crisis is "apocalyptic."

The Greek root word means "reveal" or "uncover." Apocalyptic prophecy in Scripture reveals the way the God who was at work in the past is at work in the present to fulfill God's redemptive purpose in the future. The biblical prophets challenge us to repent—meaning, to turn around—and reorient our way of living to participate in the promise of the coming of God's Kingdom. Every crisis uncovers things we failed to see or tried to avoid. They point to the way our behavior today impacts, for good or ill, our life tomorrow.

By God's grace, any crisis can become
the crucible of hope.

The compelling urgency in a crisis is to hold—or be held by—a center of certainty that is rooted in the past, provides stability in the present, and gives direction for the future. It forces us to decide what is essential and what we need to leave behind. It challenges us to take hold of a fresh vision of the end or goal toward which we are moving.

My hope is that as we explore words from the Hebrew Scriptures that guided Jesus through crucial moments along his journey, we will discover new ways in which those words will guide us. I've included *Questions for Reflection* as an invitation to pause, find your place in the story, and listen for Christ to call you to take your next step in walking with him. These questions may also be a resource for journaling or small group discussion.

No one walks the way of discipleship alone. I'm grateful for walking companions who have encouraged, critiqued, and offered helpful guidance through multiple versions of these chapters, particularly Magrey deVega, Julia Ferenac, Tom Aitken, Neil Alexander, Candace Lewis, Dan Johnson, and the brother who has been with me since we shared the same womb, John "Jack" Harnish. I make my way by walking with joyful gratitude for Martha, my wife and best editor, who has been helping me find my bearings for more than fifty years.

Our present crises will pass, but other crises are sure to come. Bad things can happen if we lose our bearings, but by God's grace, good things can happen when we find our bearings and make our way by walking along the way Jesus walked in the way that Jesus walked it.

> Through all the changing scenes of life,
> In trouble and in joy,
> The praises of my God shall still
> My heart and tongue employ.
>
> —Tate and Brady (1696)[5]

---

5. Young, *Book of Hymns*, 56.

1

Finding Your True North

Read: Mark 12:28–34, Deuteronomy 6:1–9

Curly, the rugged, weather-beaten cowboy played to perfection by Jack Parlance in the 1991 hit movie *City Slickers*, asked Mitch, the upwardly mobile, success-driven, soul-empty New York account executive played by Billy Crystal, "Do you know what the secret of life is?" Holding up a gnarled, old index finger, Curly went on, "One thing. Just one thing. You stick to that and the rest don't mean shit."

In anxious anticipation, Mitch asked, "But what is the 'one thing'?"

Curly smiled and said, "That's what you have to figure out."[1]

Sooner or later, through crises large and small, the relentless forces of reality force us to find "one thing" that will provide inner certainty and clarity of direction when the external signposts we've followed are shaken, rearranged, or taken away. Searching for bearings along the way demands that we wrestle with some unsettling questions.

What is the "one thing" that will help us find our bearings when our external signposts are taken away?

What is the center of certainty that can provide stability in disruptive and uncertain times?

1. Underwood, *City Slickers*.

How will we find what Harvard Business School professor Bill George called "True North," which he defined as "the internal compass that guides you . . . [and] represents who you are as a human being at your deepest level"?[2]

The urgency in any crisis is to find our True North, a center of certainty that is rooted in the past, provides stability in the present, and will guide us into the future. Thomas Merton, the Trappist monk whose personal search for faith continues to inspire spiritual seekers, named it as our innate need for "a certitude that goes beyond reason and beyond simple faith."[3]

Three of the four Gospels include the story of a nameless man identified as a scribe. He was a legal expert, an authority on the Scriptures. I see him as a person like many of us who in the anonymity of our own souls are searching for True North. He wanted to find "one thing" that would provide a center of certainty in the crises of his life.

> One of the legal experts heard their dispute and saw how well Jesus answered them. He came over and asked him, "Which commandment is the most important of all?" (Mark 12:28)

We enter the story at the conclusion of vigorous discussion about the fine points of the law. Perhaps this scribe was weary of spiritually vapid, intellectually exhausting debates when he stepped away from the nit-picking religious legalists and "came over" to Jesus. He spoke with the ruthless honesty of a persistent question that percolates quietly in some silent corner of the soul until it bursts into speech, "Which commandment is the most important of all?"

Questions for Reflection

What do you think brought this scribe to Jesus?

How can you identify with his search?

2. George, *True North*, xxiii.
3. Merton, *Essential Writings*, 58.

How would you define True North for your life?

Searching for Certainty

The scribe in the Gospel story wasn't alone in his search for certainty. Gil Rendle, writing as an authority on leadership in times of change, asserts that "certainty stands with convergence."[4] He pointed to the cultural convergence of the post-WWII era that provided certainty for me and for many people in my generation.

I'm a Medicare-card-carrying product of the Baby Boom generation. I grew up in the middle of the middle class, in a solidly white, politically conservative, county seat town in the hills of Western Pennsylvania. I found my bearings in the supposedly ideal family portrayed on our black-and-white television by *Ozzie and Harriett* and *Father Knows Best*. The roots of my faith were planted in the soil of white, mainline, American Methodism and what is known as the "holiness" tradition. The convergence of the culture provided unquestioned certainty for my adolescent development. I was naïve enough to be absolutely sure of just about everything!

But Rendle calls those post-WWII years an "aberrant" era when "a convergence of unique conditions creates an environment . . . that is uniquely tied to that moment but cannot continue beyond the moment that created it." He stresses that we are now in a "divergent" culture in which divergence "takes certainty away."[5]

Times have changed! Things we assumed were nailed down have been shaken loose. Ozzie and Harriet died a long time ago. Demonic powers of racism, sexism, economic injustice, and inequality that slithered beneath the surface of the *Father Knows Best* culture have been laid bare as people from outside our "convergent culture" bubble have found their voices and are once again calling our country to live up to the promise of liberty and justice for all.

While we were reeling under the impact of the coronavirus pandemic, we were brutally confronted with the virulent virus of racism that has infected our nation's bloodstream since the first

4. Rendle, *Quietly Courageous*, 34.

5. Rendle, *Quietly Courageous*, 22, 34.

slaves were unloaded on these shores four-hundred years ago. Video coverage of George Floyd dying under the knee of a white police officer forced white people to see with brutal clarity the racism that Black people have seen for generations. It opened the flood gates for massive demonstrations calling for fundamental and systemic change. The all-too-predictable backlash unleashed white supremacists carrying their guns and waving Confederate- and Nazi-emblazed flags.

At the same time, the cultural convergence rooted in an Americanized version of the Christian faith has been blown away so that "none" is the most rapidly growing religious preference among young adults. Pope Francis named the religious crisis when he declared, "*Christendom no longer exists!* . . . We are no longer living in a Christian world, because faith . . . is no longer an evident presupposition of social life." He warned of the temptation "to fall back on the past . . . because it is more reassuring, familiar, and, to be sure, less conflictual." He challenged us to avoid "a rigidity born of the fear of change, which ends up erecting fences and obstacles on the terrain of the common good, turning it into a minefield of incomprehension and hatred."[6]

There are times when I wish the Pope had been incorrect. As a pastor in a mainline denomination, I sometimes wish I were living in the era when the church was at the center of the community and everyone who was anyone came through its doors on Sunday morning.

I understand why the fear of loss and change has energized some faithful people to take a reactionary position, fighting to recapture a mythical era of greatness that others—particularly immigrants and people of color—say wasn't all that great anyway. Politically defined evangelicals believed that Donald Trump's promise to make American great *again* would recreate the Christendom culture of the 1950s in which they felt safe and secure. Meanwhile, other Christians hide away from the crisis in a cozy cocoon of personal piety that John Wesley critiqued when he declared "holy solitaries" as being "no more consistent with the

6. Francis, *Christmas Greetings*, para. 14.

gospel than holy adulterers." The founder of the Methodist movement asserted, "The gospel of Christ knows no religion, but social; no holiness but social holiness."[7]

We have good reasons to identify with the crisis in the soul of the nameless scribe in the Gospel who refused to settle for the certainty of his past. With him, we listen for Jesus' answer.

"Listen! Our God is the LORD! Only the LORD!"
(Deut 6:4)

In response to the scribe's question, Jesus reached back into the *Torah* (the first five books of the Hebrew Scripture) and drew on some of the first words he would have learned to speak as a toddler at Joseph's knee. They were words with which every faithful Israelite would greet the morning and go to sleep at night; their first words of prayer and their final words in death. No words were more deeply embedded in the hearts and minds of the Hebrew people than the *Shema,* the imperative command, "Listen!" The *Shema* was and is the center of certainty, the True North of Hebrew life and faith, the foundational affirmation of monotheistic religion: "Israel, listen! Our God is the Lord! Only the Lord!" (Deut 6:4).

I remember hearing the story of a man in New York City who, like so many patients during the coronavirus pandemic, was dying alone in a COVID-19 ICU. The nurse informed the man's son by phone that his father was nearing death. The son pleaded with the nurse to hold the phone to his father's ear, something the nurse was not permitted to do. The son was so insistent that the nurse finally gave in, held the phone to the dying man's ear, and overheard the son whisper, "*Sh'ma Yisra'eil Adonai Eloheinu Adonai echad.*"

The biblical setting for the *Shema* could not be more dramatic. The book of Deuteronomy contains the last words of Moses as he prepared the Israelites to cross the river into the Promised Land, a destination he saw in the distance from Mount Pisgah (also called Mt. Nebo) but will not enter (Deut 3:23–28). Martin Luther King Jr. recaptured that moment the night before he died when he declared,

7. Wesley, *Hymns,* viii.

"I've been to the mountaintop . . . I've seen the Promised Land. I may not get there with you. But I want you to know tonight, that we, as a people, will get to the Promised Land."[8]

Moses delivered three major addresses or sermons in Deuteronomy. In the first sermon (1:1—4:30), he looked "all the way back to the day God first created human beings on the earth" (Deut 4:32). He retold the foundational story of the way God brought the Israelites out of the "iron furnace" of slavery in Egypt (4:20), provided for them in the wilderness, facilitated their victory over hostile forces, and gave them the Ten Commandments.

In Moses' second sermon (4:44—26:28) he answered the scribe's question, "Which is most important?" when he declared, "Hear, O Israel: The Lord is our God, the Lord alone" (Deut 6:4 NRSV).

The *Shema* affirmed the absolute certainty that there is one and only one God to whom their absolute loyalty belonged. In a divergent culture that was (and still is) crowded with a pantheon of cultural gods that might draw people away from the covenant, the Lord who brought the Hebrew people out of bondage in Egypt is the only God worthy to be the center of certainty for their life and worship.

The third sermon (29:1—30:20) was Moses' soul-inspiring farewell address. He looked forcefully to the future, reiterated his instructions for their life together, commissioned Joshua to carry on his leadership, and concluded with words that continue to challenge us.

> I call heaven and earth as my witnesses against you right now: I have set life and death, blessing and curse before you. Now choose life—so that you and your descendants will live—by loving the Lord your God, by obeying his voice, and by clinging to him. That's how you will survive and live long on the fertile land the Lord swore to give to your ancestors: to Abraham, Isaac, and Jacob. (Deut 30:19–20)

Moses' farewell sermon ends with words of encouragement.

8. King, *Testament of Hope*, 286.

Be strong! Be fearless! Don't be afraid and don't be scared by your enemies, because the Lord your God is the one who marches with you. He won't let you down, and he won't abandon you. (Deut 31:6–8)

Paul Young captured the spirit of the *Shema* for followers of Christ in *The Shack* when Jesus tells the novel's central character:

Mack, I don't want to be first among a list of values; I want to be at the center of everything. When I live in you, then together we can live through everything that happens to you . . . I want to be the center of a mobile, where everything in your life—your friends, family, occupation, thoughts, activities—is connected to me . . . in an incredible dance of being.[9]

Questions for Reflection

How does the setting of Moses' command impact your understanding of the Shema?

In a "divergent culture," what are the "other gods" that might attract your loyalty?

What does Moses' command mean for your life as a follower of Christ?

"Love the Lord your God with all your heart, all your being, and all your strength." (Deut 6:5)

Jesus continued by recalling the imperative command that is the only appropriate response to who God is and what God has done: "Love the Lord your God with all your heart, all your being, and all your strength" (Deut 6:5). It is repeated five times in Deuteronomy (11:1,13, 22; 13:3; 30:6).

9. Young, *Shack*, 207.

Paul proclaimed the same life-centering love when he affirmed God's act of love for us and our response of love for God. He declared that God's liberating, love-defining, history-shaping "Yes" in Jesus calls for an equally life-shaping "Yes" from us and an equally emphatic "No" to any other gods and every other power or authority that would attempt to draw us away from this one God who is the only one worthy of our loyalty and love (2 Cor 1:16–20).

We can hear the challenge of Moses in Deuteronomy and Paul in Corinthians in words that Dietrich Bonhoeffer preached to his confirmation class while Hitler was coalescing his power in Germany.

> From now on either you serve God alone or you do not serve God at all. Now you only have *one* Lord, who is the Lord of the world, who is the Savior of the World . . . But to this Yes to God belongs an equally clear No. Your Yes to God demands your No to all injustice, to all evil, to all lies, to all oppression and violation of the weak and the poor . . . Your Yes to God demands a brave No to everything that will ever hinder you from serving God alone.[10]

When Jesus triggered the memory of Moses' words in the minds of his hearers, he set the biblical understanding of God's love for us and of our love for God as True North for this scribe's life. But he didn't stop there. He went on, "The second is like it" (Matt 22:39). If love for God is the most important commandment, there is an inseparable and equally important command for that same love to become a tangible reality in our human relationships. Jesus didn't invent the second commandment often called the "Golden Rule"; he reclaimed it from the book of Leviticus.

"You will love your neighbor as yourself." (Lev 19:18)

Well-intended people who set out to read the Bible beginning with Genesis and Exodus often give up somewhere in Leviticus, with its detailed laws for everything from burnt offerings to menstrual

---

10. Bonhoeffer, *Collected Sermons*, 203.

cycles. They invariably throw their hands in the air and ask, "What should we do with this stuff?"

A. J. Jacobs, who described himself as being Jewish in the way that Olive Garden is an Italian restaurant, narrated his attempt to practice the Levitical laws in his best-selling book, *The Year of Living Biblically: One Man's Humble Quest to Follow the Bible as Literally as Possible*. He discovered that some rules are "startlingly relevant" while others "baffle the 21st century brain." In the process he confirmed that "literalism is not the best way to interpret the Bible."[11]

We don't need to take Leviticus literally in order to take it seriously. The detailed laws in Leviticus were culturally conditioned practices by which the Hebrew people ordered their relationships with God and each other to obey the central command, "You must be holy, because I, the Lord your God, am holy" (Lev 19:2). Paul Chilcote and Steve Harper refer to the Old Testament laws as "enacted love."[12] The laws were the concrete, down-to-earth behaviors through which God's holy love was intended to permeate the way they lived their personal lives and the way they lived together in community.

We will hear Jesus reinterpret the Levitical call to holiness in the Sermon on the Mount (Matt 5:17–48), but for this scribe (and for us) Jesus linked together the commands to love God and to love others as the magnetic pole around which everything else revolves.

The love with which Jesus calls us to love others is nothing other than love defined by the God who loves us. Jesus underscored that connection on the night before he died when he told his disciples, "As the Father loved me, I too have loved you . . . This is my commandment: love each other just as I have loved you" (John 15:9–12). The writer of the Epistle of John applied those words directly to our human relationships.

---

11. Jacobs, *Living Biblically*, 257.
12. Chilcote, *Living Hope*, 4.

This is love: it is not that we loved God but that he loved us and sent his Son as the sacrifice that deals with our sins . . . if God loved us this way, we also ought to love each other . . . This commandment we have from him: Those who claim to love God ought to love their brother and sister also. (1 John 4:10–21)

There's no easy escape from the disconcerting way Jesus binds love of God and love of neighbor together. It disrupts every attempt to separate belief from behavior, spirituality from practice, or faith in Christ from our social, economic, and political lives. But how is that love acted out in real human relationships? Jesus' answer to the legal expert's question led to the follow-up question every inquiring disciple wants to ask.

"Who is my neighbor?" (Luke 10:29)

In responding to the question, Jesus didn't give a simple, twenty-five-words-or-fewer definition. As he often did, he told a story.

The story of the Good Samaritan (Luke 10:30–37) is worn thin by familiarity, but it continues to wear well. It's Jesus' dramatic portrayal of the love of God becoming a flesh-and-blood reality in costly, life-giving, concrete compassion for others, specifically for people in need; particularly in relationships that cross the boundaries of race, status, and culture. We watched this parable became a reality in the exhausting, relentless compassion demonstrated by the doctors, nurses, emergency workers, and care givers who, at risk to their own health, cared for COVID-19 patients in over-crowded ICU units.

I was intrigued by another biblical enactment of the commandment when the Revised Common Lectionary linked Mark's version of Jesus' commandment with the story of a woman named Ruth, a story that was polished to perfection in the oral tradition long before it was written down. It was the kind of story Jesus must have heard repeated by storytellers in the Nazareth community.

A Hebrew woman named Naomi is left destitute in the foreign country of Moab after the deaths of her husband and sons.

She is a poor, helpless victim of a patriarchal culture, just as help-less in her own way as the man who fell among thieves on his way from Jerusalem to Jericho. Enter her daughter-in-law, a Moabite woman named Ruth. Like the Samaritan in Jesus' parable, Ruth is a non-Jew, an outsider to the covenant, an alien to the Hebrew culture and religious tradition.

Naomi's only option is to return to her hometown in Beth-lehem in the hope that a male relative will provide for her. She's not unlike the desperate immigrants who wait at the border with Mexico in the hope of being received into the United States. She pleads with Ruth to stay in Moab to find another husband, but in one of the most courageously tender scenes in Scripture, Ruth declares her loyalty and love for Naomi.

> Do not press me to leave you
> or to turn back from following you!
> Where you go, I will go;
> where you lodge, I will lodge;
> your people shall be my people,
> and your God my God.
> May the LORD do thus and so to me,
> and more as well,
> if even death parts me from you! (Ruth 1:16–17 NRSV)

The Hebrew storyteller points out that this exchange between Ruth and Naomi happens "along the road" (1:7). Imaginative readers might hear a subtle parallel in the way the Samaritan picked up a helpless victim along the Jericho road, bound up his wounds, and took him to the inn.

Ruth and Naomi return to Bethlehem where, with clever guidance from her mother-in-law, Ruth marries a Hebrew man named Boaz and they have a son. When the child is presented to Naomi, the women of the community speak words to her that could also be spoken to the man who was rescued by the Samari-tan, "May the Lord be blessed, who today hasn't left you without a redeemer" (4:14). Ruth's story ends with a hint of the future when the storyteller says, "They called his name Obed. He became Jesse's father and David's grandfather" (4:17).

Reading backward, our memory leaps across the generations when Luke locates Jesus' birth in Bethlehem, which was Naomi's hometown, and includes Obed, David's grandfather, in the genealogy of Jesus (Luke 3:23–38). Luke's genealogy places the faithful loyalty, steadfast love, and active compassion of David's great grandmother, a Moabite woman named Ruth, in the direct line that leads to Jesus' story of the Samaritan's compassion for the man on the side of the road. Both stories demonstrate the way the love of God that became flesh in Jesus becomes a flesh-and-blood reality through active, costly, self-giving compassion for others.

In Mark's version of the gospel, the certainty-seeking scribe was blown away by Jesus' words. He responded, "Well said, Teacher." He instinctively knew that loving God and loving others are "much more important than all kinds of entirely burned offerings and sacrifices" (Mark 12:32). Loving God and loving others became the "one thing," the center of certainty for which he had been searching.

Thomas Merton had a similar experience shortly after he entered the Abbey of Gethsemani. He was walking through the shopping district at the corner of Fourth and Walnut in Louisville, Kentucky, when loving God and loving people connected for him.

> I was suddenly overwhelmed with the realization that I loved all those people, that they were mine and I theirs, that we could not be alien to one another even though we were total strangers. It was like waking from a dream of separateness, of spurious self-isolation . . . This sense of liberation from an illusory difference was such a relief and such a joy to me that I almost laughed out loud . . . I have the immense joy of being man, a member of a race in which God Himself became incarnate.[13]

Both the scribe in the Gospel story and Thomas Merton on the street in Louisville found their bearings in loving God and loving others. We name Jesus' combination of words from Deuteronomy

13. Merton, *Essential Writings*, 38.

and Leviticus as the Great (or Greatest) Commandment, because it really is!

Questions for Reflection

Where do you find yourself in Jesus' story of the Good Samaritan (Luke 10:30–37)?

How does Ruth's story provide a fresh perspective on "the Golden Rule"?

What difference does the commandment to love God and love others make in the way you respond to issues such as racism, health care, and immigration?

"Get Going!" (Deut 1:6)

Mt. Horeb, also known as Mt. Sinai or "Mountain of *YHWH* [the Lord]," is the dramatic site of Moses' final words in Deuteronomy. It was where he received the Ten Commandments and the laws and practices that would be True North for the Hebrew people. Mt. Horeb was also where God, in no uncertain terms, declared, "You've been at this mountain long enough. Get going!" (Deut 1:6). The command to "get going" appears six times in Deuteronomy. It's God's command for the Israelites to take action—to move on toward the Promised Land.

Because Matthew's Gospel was addressed to or emerged from a predominantly Jewish community, it should come as no surprise that mountains are decisive locations in that Gospel. On a mountain, the disciples receive the core of Jesus' teachings in the Sermon on the Mount (Matt 5:1–48). On another mountain, Peter, James, and John experience the Transfiguration (Matt 17:1), which connects Jesus directly with Elijah and Moses. In the grand finale of the Gospel, Matthew takes us to another mountain where we hear the reverberation of Moses' command to "Get going!" in the words we have come to know as the Great Commission.

"I've received all authority in heaven and on earth.
Therefore, go and make disciples of all nations, baptizing
them in the name of the Father and of the Son and of the
Holy Spirit, teaching them to obey everything that I've
commanded you. Look, I myself will be with you every
day until the end of this present age." (Matt 28:18–20)

The Great Commission could not be clearer: Go, make disciples!
Go, baptize! Go, teach! Go, in the authority of the Risen Christ!
Don't just stand there, do something! Get going!

When the General Conference of the United Methodist
Church voted to declare that the mission of the church is "making disciples of Jesus Christ for the transformation of the world,"
the genetically inherited cynic in me snarked, "It's about time!
I'm sure Jesus will be pleased that we finally got around to doing
what he told us to do two-thousand years ago!" But my inner
cynic was wrong. Like other congregations around the globe,
that mission statement prodded the congregation I was serving to ask some basic questions about our ministry. How were
we fulfilling that mission? What was the process by which we
could meet people wherever they are on their spiritual journey
and invite them to take their next appropriate step in becoming
disciples and participating in God's transformation of the world?
How would we, as Methodists, fulfill the Great Commission in a
uniquely Wesleyan way?

Our response to those questions began with the foundational question, "What is a disciple?" While there are a variety
of biblically appropriate answers, our team returned to Jesus' response to the scribe who was searching for True North. We found
our bearings in Jesus' answer to his question and said, "A disciple
is a follower of Jesus whose life is centering on loving God and
loving others."[14] We chose the active verb "centering" because
in the Wesleyan tradition, being transformed into a follower of
Jesus who loves God and loves others is an ongoing process of
God's grace at work within us throughout our lives. God never

14. Harnish, Disciple's Path, 17.

stops loving, and we never stop growing in what it means to love God and love others.

The Great Commandment is the goal or end toward which our discipleship is leading as we become people who love God with our whole heart, mind, soul, and strength, and who love others the way they have been loved by God. The Great Commission compels us to go into the world to invite others to become disciples and to participate with us in God's transformation of the kingdoms of this earth into the Kingdom of God (Rev 11:15).

The good news is that along with the command, "Get going!" we receive Jesus' promise, "Look, I myself will be with you every day until the end of this present age" (Matt 28:20). He offers us the same assurance that Moses promised to the Israelites, "Don't be terrified! Don't be afraid . . . The LORD your God is going before you" (Deut 1:29–30).

Responding to the Great Commandment and participating in the Great Commission called for creative action during the COVID-19 crisis. For most congregations, it meant developing new ways of using technology and social networks to participate in worship and be connected in Christian community. The crisis compelled a congregation located near a major medical center to reach out to medical teams to pray specifically for them and to support their families. At the height of the crisis, they lined the sidewalk from the parking lot to the ER entrance to cheer for the medical staff during their shift change.

In another congregation, a group of older women who found community in gathering together to sew dresses for a mission project in Africa began meeting online as they sewed face masks for school children in underprivileged neighborhoods. A volunteer team made telephone calls at least once a week to church members in nursing homes or who lived alone as an act of caring for them. A congregation serving the Walt Disney World and Universal Studio communities provided food for musicians, artists, and performers who were out of work. Others wrestled deeply with the relentless reality of white supremacy and confronted the exponential impact of the crisis on minority populations. Others lobbied Congress for expanded access to health care. Others joined massive marches to call for social justice. Across the nation, simply wearing a mask became a tangible way of loving our neighbors.

Followers of Jesus who have found their True North in the Great Commandment and their calling in the Great Commission are instructed by the Risen Christ to "Get going!" in the assurance that, just as Moses promised the Israelites, God is going with them.

Questions for Reflection

How have you heard God say, "Get going!"

What are you doing to continue centering your life in loving God and loving others?

What are the next appropriate steps for you to take to respond to the Great Commission?

2

Wrestling in the Wilderness

Read: Luke 3:21–22, 4:1–13, Matthew 4:1–11

The wilderness is a terrible place to lose our bearings. But it can also be the place where we find God, find ourselves, and find our bearings for the rest of our journey.

Erik Kulick is the founder of True North Wilderness Survival School. He teaches people who are heading into the wilderness that "survival isn't really so much about how much gear you have in your backpack. Rather, in any survival situation, it's what's in your head and heart that most matters."[1] Every crisis forces us to wrestle with what matters most in our head and heart.

What is essential for our living?

What marks the boundary between what we want and what we need?

How do we determine the way we follow and the way in which we follow it?

How will we deal with temptations to choose an easier way?

If we are following the way Jesus followed God's call for his life, those are the kind of soul-level, survival issues we confront in

---

1. Kulick, *True North*, para. 2.

the wilderness. Answering those questions marks the way we find our bearings.

> "The Spirit immediately drove him out into the
> wilderness. He was in the wilderness forty days."
> (Mark 1:12–13 NRSV)

If there was ever a place where Jesus might have lost his bearings, it could have been during the forty long, hot days and cold, lonely nights he spent in the dry, barren wilderness. Throughout Scripture, references to "forty days" and the "wilderness" conjure up the memory of the Israelites's forty-year journey through the wilderness, the forty days Noah spent in the ark, or the forty days Moses and Elijah each spent alone with God on Mt. Horeb.

The story of Jesus' forty days in the wilderness is strategically located between his baptism and the beginning of his ministry. The Gospel writers are not interested in locating the wilderness on a map, but about tracking the wilderness in the terrain of Jesus' soul.

It was a place of testing where, in the naked reality of his humanity, Jesus was stripped of every false identity that would compete with the identity God had announced at his baptism.

It was a place of temptation where he was forced to choose the way by which he would follow the way to which God had called him.

It was the place of self-examination where Jesus prepared his head and heart to walk the way that would lead to a cross.

It's our story, too. Sooner rather than later and more than just once, people who are walking the way Jesus walked in the way he walked it find themselves in that lonely place of the soul where we wrestle with "what's in [our] head and heart that most matters." Our temptations are generally less dramatic than the accounts of Jesus' experience, but they are just as determinative for our journey as Jesus' decisions were for his.

The Gospel writers agree that Jesus went to the wilderness to be tempted ("tested") by the power of evil identified in

Scripture and tradition by many names: Satan, Devil, Lucifer, Prince of Darkness, Beelzebub, Mephistopheles, Old Scratch. C. S. Lewis introduced us to Screwtape, the Senior Tempter who, in *The Screwtape Letters*, instructs his nephew, Wormwood, in the most effective ways to tempt his human subject away from their Enemy, who is, of course, God. By any name, Satan is the personification of inner and external forces that would lure us away from God's will and way. Satan's goal in the wilderness was to cause Jesus to lose his bearings, to turn him away from the way God was calling him to go.

Mark used a forceful Greek verb to say that the Spirit "drove" or "forced" Jesus away from the calm waters of the Jordan River into the rugged desert of the wilderness. The same Spirit who descended like a dove with the words of assurance, "You are my Son, whom I dearly love" (Mark 1:11), now dove like a hawk, forcing Jesus to go where he would not have chosen to go. The wilderness is not usually where we choose to go either!

Sometimes we are driven into the wilderness by circumstances over which we have no control: a pandemic that encircles the globe, disruptive social change that causes us to surrender our position of preference or power, the humiliation of moral failure, a career that evaporated in an economic decline, a relationship that was unintentionally fractured, a body camera image of a Black man under a white officer's knee that forces us to face systemic racism we had tried to ignore, the death of someone we loved. Changes over which we have no control take us to places we would not choose to go.

Sometimes we are driven by what Martin Luther King Jr. called "a divine dissatisfaction"[2] with the way things are in the world around us. Followers of Jesus become dissatisfied with the economic injustice, environmental destruction, subtle sexism, and political polarization around us. When we ask, "God, why don't you do something about this?" all too often we hear God reply, "That's my question for you!"

2. King, *Testament of Hope*, 251.

Sometimes the Spirit drives us deeper into the wilderness to confront sins of both omission and commission. During the crises of 2020, many of us were challenged by Ibram X. Kendi's best-selling book, *How to Be an Anti-Racist*. He compares the way we deal with racism to fighting an addiction, requiring "persistent self-awareness, constant self-criticism, and regular self-examination."[3]

Sometimes we are driven by a gnawing hunger for something more. We grow tired of life that has become stale, uninteresting, or just plain boring. We instinctively know that God has something better for us and for our world. For reasons we can neither explain nor escape, we find ourselves in a soul-level wilderness where we wrestle with what is in our head and heart—the things that matter most.

Questions for Reflection

Why do you think Jesus' temptation came "immediately" after his baptism?

When have you been driven to your own wilderness experience?

What are the surprising hungers in your life?

"Since you are God's Son . . ." (Matt 4:3)

The Tempter never questions what happened when Jesus came up out of the water of baptism, saw the Spirit descend like a dove, and heard a voice from heaven that declared, "This is my Son whom I dearly love" (Matt 3:16–17). He doesn't debate John's identification of Jesus as "the Lamb of God who takes away the sin of the world" (John 1:29). Satan never refutes the end or purpose of Jesus' ministry and mission. Instead, Satan taunts him, "*Since* you're God's Son, act like it! Use some of that God-like power to make good things happen! Do it my way! And do it now!" The temptations are

3. Kendi, *Anti-Racist*, 23.

focused not on who Jesus is but on the way he will follow the way God has called him to go. Satan's tests are around the means by which Jesus will be who God declared him to be, not the mission to which he had been called.

We know the common, everyday temptations that slither up from the dark, sin-infected instincts of our fallen humanity. The writer of the Epistle of James pointed to us in confessing, "Everyone is tempted by their own cravings; they are lured away and enticed by them" (Jas 1:14–15). The "seven deadly sins" that we try to deny—pride, envy, gluttony, greed, lust, sloth, wrath—are very much alive in and among us.

By contrast, Jesus' temptations are the more sinister kind that corrupt our highest ideals and undermine our best intentions. He was not tempted to do bad things, but to do good things in a bad way; to do God's work in ways that were not consistent with God's character; to attempt to bring in the Kingdom of God through less-than-Kingdom-shaped means; to accomplish God's saving purpose without following the way of God's self-giving love.

Where did Jesus—where do we—find strength to overcome every form of temptation? How did Jesus find the way through the wilderness without losing his bearings? How can we? If we follow Jesus' way, we learn to *remember*.

Jesus remembered Moses' call to the Israelites to remember their journey through the wilderness. By remembering God's action in the past, Jesus found "the internal compass . . . [his] orienting point" that enabled him to "stay on track"[4] when he might have been diverted from the way God had called him to go. Following his way through the wilderness invites us to remember those stories, too.

"Command these stones to become bread." (Matt 4:3)

Matthew says that "after Jesus had fasted for forty days and forty nights, he was starving" (Matt 4:2). Who wouldn't be? The testing begins with our most basic human need for food.

4. George, *True North*, xxiii.

It's no small thing that the wilderness story finds the incarnate Son of God experiencing the starvation that millions of people around the globe face every day. The story ends with Jesus' cry from the cross, "I thirst!" (John 19:28). To call Jesus *Immanuel* ("God with us") is to say that God is present in and with every person whose famished body cries out for food or water. When we enter into their suffering, we often discover the presence of the "Suffering Servant" (Isa 52:13—53:12) and are challenged to respond.

Even if we've never faced physical starvation, we know how it feels to be starved of physical and emotional strength. COVID-19 isolation took us to lonely, dry places where our souls were famished. Managing the impact of "coronavirus anxiety," social media saturation, and frustration with each day's "breaking news" headlines left us worn out! Times of emotional and physical exhaustion can easily become the times when we are tempted to turn in on ourselves, away from others, and away from our awareness of the presence and purpose of God.

St. Augustine described our condition with the Latin phrase *incurvatus in se,* the soul "turned in on itself." Martin Luther, the sixteenth-century Reformer, said our human nature is "so deeply curved in on itself that it . . . bends the best gifts of God toward itself."[5] It's the sinful self-addiction C. S. Lewis named as "the ruthless, sleepless, unsmiling concentration upon self which is the mark of Hell."[6]

I sometimes think of *incurvatus in se* when I take a *selfie*. The person taking the picture is in the center with everyone and everything else in the background. It's a small symptom of a deadly addiction. We are enticed by a tenacious narcissism that drives us to satisfy our own needs without regard to the needs of others. We saw it during the pandemic when some people refused to wear a mask because they thought it impinged on their personal freedom with no concern of the risk of infecting people around them. With

5. Luther, *Lectures on Romans*, quoted in Johnston, *Saving God*, 88.

6. Lewis, *Screwtape Letters*, 5.

Jesus in the wilderness, we are tempted to bend God's best gifts to our own self-serving ends.

It's not as if Jesus didn't have the power to turn stones into bread. All four Gospels tell the story of the way he miraculously fed thousands of hungry people (Matt 14:13–21; Mark 6:30–44; Luke 9:10–17; John 6:1–15). Every inquiring mind wants to ask, why didn't Jesus use just a little bit of that God-given power to provide bread for his famished body?

"People don't live by bread alone." (Deut 8:2)

In his hunger-induced imagination, Jesus remembered Moses' interpretation of the way God was at work in the lives of the people through their experience of hunger in the wilderness.

> Remember the long road on which the Lord your God led you during these forty years in the desert so he could humble you, testing you to find out what was in your heart: whether you would keep his commandments or not. He humbled you by making you hungry and then feeding you the manna that neither you nor your ancestors had ever experienced, so he could teach you that people don't live on bread alone. No, they live based on whatever the Lord says. (Deut 8:2–3)

Jesus was not simply quoting Scripture as a magical totem to ward off temptation. As he remembered "the long road" the Israelites traveled he must have experienced the humility of being hungry. In his imagination he could taste the manna that God provided for starving, helpless people on their circuitous way.

Jesus' rejection of the temptation to use God's gifts for his own needs is the reminder that although food is essential for human survival, it's not enough to live on. Perhaps he recalled this temptation when he said, "There is more to life than food and more to the body than clothing" (Luke 12:23).

We are made for more than mere physical survival or the satisfaction of the narcissistic instincts of our self-absorbed, sin-infected humanity. The deepest hunger of our human hearts is for the life-giving, spirit-nourishing presence of the living God that is, in fact, "The bread of God . . . who comes down from heaven and gives life to the world" (John 6:33). Paul prescribed his cure for our *selfie* addiction when he wrote:

> Now the way we live is based on the Spirit, not based on selfishness. People whose lives are based on selfishness think about selfish things, but people whose lives are based on the Spirit think about things that are related to the Spirit. The attitude that comes from selfishness leads to death, but the attitude that comes from the Spirit leads to life and peace. (Rom 8:4–6)

A life turned in on itself becomes smaller and smaller until there is nothing left but its own insatiable, self-consuming hunger. But a healthy, whole, abundant life is the result of hearing and following the way of Jesus that turns our attention away from ourselves and toward God's self-giving life and love, the love that can nourish our parched, starving souls.

Questions for Reflection

When have you known the hunger described here?

How have you experienced the "tenacious narcissism" that places yourself at the center of everything?

How do Paul's words from Romans speak to your experience?

> "Throw yourself down; for it is written, I will command my angels concerning you, and they will take you up in their hands so that you won't hit your foot on a stone."
> (Matt 4:6)

In Screwtape's toast at the Annual Dinner of the Tempters Training College, he instructs the young tempters, "The fine flower of unholiness can grow only in the close neighborhood of the Holy. Nowhere do we tempt so successfully as on the very steps of the altar."[7] So, Satan took Jesus "into the holy city and stood him at the highest point of the temple." There was no holier place. Then the Tempter quoted Scripture.

You've probably noticed that just about anyone can quote the Bible for just about any reason. Satan was neither the first nor the last to use Scripture to defend attitudes and actions that are brazenly inconsistent with the character of God revealed in the written word and made flesh in Jesus. Abraham Lincoln got it right when he looked out on a nation divided by the Civil War and said, "Both read the same Bible, and pray to the same God; and each invokes His aid against the other."[8]

I stand in the line of Methodist preachers who prayed to the same God, preached from the same Bible, and divided the church over slavery in 1844. As I write, the United Methodist Church is again being divided by people who quote the same Bible and pray to the same God but come to opposing convictions about marriage and ordination of LGBTQ persons. My own denomination's history decisively disproves the simplistic mantra, "The Bible said it! I believe it! That settles it!" Even Satan uses Scripture for his self-absorbed purpose. He tempted Jesus by quoting Psalm 91:3–13:

> Because you've made the Lord my refuge,
>
> the Most High, your place of residence—
>
> no evil will happen to you;
>
> no disease will come close to your tent.
>
> Because he will order his messengers to help you,
>
> to protect you wherever you go.
>
> They will carry you with their own hands
>
> so you don't bruise your foot on a stone.

Jesus must have heard those words in the synagogue in Nazareth. Perhaps Mary and Joseph sang that psalm at home or recited those words as they fled from Bethlehem to seek political asylum in Egypt. As a person who grew up hearing and singing hymns at

7. Lewis, *Screwtape Letters*, 185.

8. Lincoln, "Second Inaugural."

home and in the church, the words of those hymns are so deeply imbedded in my memory that I instinctively hear their refrains in times of soul-lifting gratitude or heart-breaking pain. Perhaps Jesus recalled this psalm in the same way.

Satan, the creator of nothing but the manipulator of anything, took words that were already alive in Jesus' mind and heart and twisted them to his purpose. I hear the Tempter proposing, "So, you believe that promise, do you? So, prove it! How about taking an Olympic-winning high dive to demonstrate the power of God?"

The temptation presumed that by leaping from the Temple, Jesus could force God's power for his own advantage. It's a temptation that is very much alive among us. It's the devilish notion that God's power is demonstrated by prayerful pyrotechnics through which we can force God's hand to give us whatever we think we want or need.

Sometimes I'm tempted to use the psalm the way Satan did.

Sometimes I'd like to have a God who shows up on call to do what I want God to do.

Sometimes I wish God were like Superman in the 1950s TV series I grew up watching on our black-and-white television. Superman always showed up just in time to rescue Lois Lane and Jimmy Olsen.

Sometimes I pray that God would magically blow away the coronavirus pandemic, instantly heal all who are infected, and miraculously resolve the political, economic, and racial divisions that are tearing our nation apart.

But Jesus didn't take the bait. He didn't do a high dive from the pinnacle of the Temple. Rather, he found strength in remembering Moses saying, "Don't test the Lord your God the way you frustrated him at Massah" (Deut 6:16).

Moses' words conjure up the disconcerting memory of what happened at Massah and Meribah (Exod 17:1–7). The precise location is unknown. The names may be imaginary. The words mean "testing" and "quarreling." The quarreling was over the need for water. The testing was whether God could be trusted to provide it. On God's instruction, Moses struck the rock and the water flowed.

Massah and Meribah became the disquieting reminder of the Israelites's rebellion against God and of the way God provided for them in spite of it. We hear the warning in the Psalm 95:

> Don't harden your hearts
>
> like you did at Meribah,
>
> like you did when you were at Massah,
>
> in the wilderness,
>
> when your ancestors tested me
>
> and scrutinized me,
>
> even though they had already seen my acts. (Ps 95:6–8)

We confront the same temptation as the Israelites who "argued with and tested the Lord, asking, 'Is the Lord really with us or not?'" (Exod 17:7). Would Jesus—and can we—trust that God is with us and that God will provide our deepest needs without spectacular signs of power but with the assurance of God's presence? Could God's presence be enough to see us through the wilderness? God gets the last word in the psalm:

> Whenever you cry out to me, I'll answer.
>
> I'll be with you in troubling times.
>
> I'll save you and glorify you.
>
> I'll show you my salvation. (Ps 91:14–16)

For Jesus, that promise was enough to see him through the temptation. William Sloane Coffin Jr. wrote, "Christ is not God's magic incarnate, but God's love incarnate."[9] Christ lives among us, not as a magician who defeats every evil or overcomes every kind of suffering with impressive displays of super-spiritual power. Instead, the Risen Christ lives among us as the assurance of God's presence with us and God's Spirit within us to enable us "to stand [our] ground on the evil day and after [we] have done everything possible to still stand" (Eph 6:13).

---

9. Coffin, *Living the Truth*, 93.

Martin Luther King Jr. experienced that assurance in the kitchen of the small, white-framed parsonage in Montgomery, Alabama:

> I couldn't sleep. It seemed that all of my fears had come down on me at once . . . I went to the kitchen and heated a pot of coffee. I was ready to give up . . . With my head in my hands, I bowed over the kitchen table and prayed aloud . . . "Lord, I'm down here trying to do what's right . . . But Lord, I must confess that I'm weak now . . . I'm losing my courage . . . I have nothing left . . . I can't face it alone."
>
> It seemed as though I could hear the quiet assurance of an inner voice saying: "Martin Luther King, stand up for righteousness. Stand up for justice. Stand up for truth. And lo, I will be with you."
>
> I heard the voice of Jesus saying still to fight on. He promised never to leave me alone. At that moment I experienced the presence of the Divine as I had never experienced Him before. Almost at once my fears began to go. My uncertainty disappeared. I was ready to face anything.[10]

Questions for Reflection

How do you deal with differing interpretations of Scripture?

When have you wished that God would do what you wanted?

What does it mean for you to hear God's promise to be with you even if you don't see spectacular evidence of it?

"I'll give you all these [kingdoms of the world] if you bow down and worship me." (Matt 4:9)

Satan sneered, "Jesus, have I got a deal for you! I'll give you all the kingdoms [empires] of the world and all their glory!" It was the temptation to use worldly power to reach a heavenly goal, to create

10. King, *Autobiography*, 77–78.

God's Kingdom by less-than-Kingdom means. But it sounds like an offer Jesus shouldn't refuse!

It would be the shortcut to the promise that one day the kingdoms of this earth shall actually become the Kingdom of God (Rev 11:15).

It would be quicker than planting mustard seeds or dropping yeast in a mixing bowl (Matt 13:32–33).

It would be more efficient than healing one blind beggar at a time (John 9:1) or feeding five-thousand people on a hillside (Matt 14:21).

It would have more hope of success than sending a bunch of demonstrably weak disciples to make disciples of all people (Matt 28:16–20).

We might ask, "Jesus, wouldn't this be a better way to fulfill your mission than going to a cross?"

History is littered with the wreckage of movements that attempted to establish the Kingdom of God by political, military, or economic power. When Timothy Egan walked from Canterbury to Rome along the *Via Francigena*, he found the relics of the bloody conflicts in which Christians slaughtered other Christians for theological, ideological, or nationalistic purposes.

At the beginning of our nation's story, pilgrims who escaped religious persecution in Europe came to the New World to build what John Winthrop eloquently envisioned as "a city on a hill." But when the formerly persecuted people acquired power, they soon became the persecutors of people who did not obey their strict religious practices or outliers like Roger Williams and Anne Hutchinson.

In the 1930s, many faithful German Christians believed that Adolf Hitler had been sent by God to make Germany great again after the defeat and humiliation of World War I. In the political crises of 2020, "evangelicals" supported Donald Trump in spite of ways in which his personal behavior and public policies contradicted their long-held values because they were convinced that God had chosen him to be their President and protector.

When will we ever learn that when faith is married to political power, political power always wins and faith becomes either an abused spouse or a prostitute? When Christians fall for the temptation to accomplish God's purpose by means that are inconsistent with God's way, it always works out badly and you can hear Satan snickering in the shadows. That's why Martin Luther King Jr. insisted that the means we use must be consistent with the end we seek. That's why John Lewis never stopped acting in ways that were consistent with the vision of the "beloved community." That's why Christ's followers are inevitably political but never partisan. They bear witness to the way every political system is accountable to the values of the Kingdom of God and the way every human institution stands under both the judgement and the mercy of God.

The problem with Satan's temptation was the fine print in the contact: ". . . if you will bow down and worship me." The choice for Jesus was clear. Would he worship God or worship Satan? Would he fulfill God's mission in God's way or the Devil's way? Would he choose the way of the reign and rule of God or would he go the way of the "principalities and powers" of this world (Eph 6:12 KJV)? I suspect he could remember the voice of Joshua, declaring, "Choose this day whom you will serve" (Josh 24:15 NRSV).

The choice of king and kingdom, who or what we will worship, is the underlying tension throughout Matthew's Gospel from King Herod in the beginning to Pilate at the end. It comes into sharp focus when Jesus says, "No one can serve two masters. Either you will hate the one and love the other, or you will be loyal to the one and have contempt for the other" (Matt 6:24). The insistent question is which king or kingdom we will serve.

In his rebuttal to Satan, Jesus again evoked the voice of Moses. "Don't forget the Lord, who brought you out of Egypt, out of the house of slavery. Revere the Lord your God, serve him . . . Don't follow other gods, those gods of the people around you" (Deut 6:12–14). Jesus blew off this temptation even more decisively than the others with a forceful command, "Go away, Satan, because it's written, you will worship the Lord your God and serve only him" (Matt 4:10). The choice was made; Jesus knew the way he would go.

Jesus responded just as decisively to Peter whom Jesus had promised would be the "rock" upon which his church would be built. When Jesus predicted his rejection and death, Peter "took hold of Jesus and, scolding him, began to correct him: 'God forbid, Lord! This won't happen to you.'" We need to give Peter credit for having the nerve to scold his Master! But Jesus rejected Peter just as forcefully as he rejected Satan. "He turned to Peter and said, 'Get behind me, Satan. You are a stone that could make me stumble, for you are not thinking God's thoughts but human thoughts'" (Matt 16:22–23).

Don't miss the contrasting metaphors of Peter as the rock on which the church would be built and the stone over which Jesus might have stumbled. The choice Jesus made in the wilderness was reaffirmed in his rebuke of Peter. Jesus had found his bearings. He would follow God's way in God's way, regardless of what was ahead.

In the wilderness, Jesus repudiated each temptation with unflinching, gut-level honesty. He broke the power of temptation with truth.

When my long-time friend and colleague, Dan Johnson, reflected on four decades of life together in our clergy retreat group, he remembered that each time we get together someone is going through a wilderness experience, either personally or professionally. He wrote, "In the naming of the pain or the hurt or the sin or the temptation, we take away its power!" He called it "the most liberating thing in the world!"

That kind of liberation can happen by speaking the truth with a spouse or friend, in a small group, or with a therapist. Without it, Dan acknowledged that "the inner temptation or pain goes further underground and festers and gathers an army around it and overpowers you from within."[11] The journey of discipleship always leads through the wilderness where we confront temptation with brutal honesty and discover God's liberating grace.

11. Robinson, *Misty Mornings*, 154.

The Tempter wasn't finished in the wilderness. Jesus confronted him again in Gethsemane when he prayed, "My Father, if it's possible, take this cup of suffering away from me. However—not what I want but what you want" (Matt 16:39). Each time the Tempter came, Jesus chose to follow God's way in God's way, the way of self-giving love rather than the way of self-serving protection.

> "The devil left him, and angels came and took
> care of him." (Matt 4:11)

C. S. Lewis unmasked Screwtape's machinations when he wrote, "We never find the strength of the evil impulse inside us until we try to fight it: and Christ, because He was the only man who never yielded to temptation, is also the only man who knows to the full what temptation means."[12] Lewis was restating the assurance of the writer of Hebrews who said, "We don't have a high priest who can't sympathize with our weaknesses but instead one who was tempted in every way that we are, except without sin" (Heb 4:15).

Luke's account of Jesus' time in the wilderness ends, "The devil departed from him *until the next opportunity*" (Luke 4:13; emphasis mine). It's at least to say that we don't get away with only one time of testing. The Tempter never quits. When Jesus was on the cross, he heard the Tempter's voice again when one of the criminals beside him asked, "Aren't you the Christ? Save yourself and us!" (Luke 23:39). One final time, Jesus rejected the temptation by drawing strength from the Psalms when he prayed, "Father, into your hands I entrust my life" (Luke 23:46; Ps 31:5).

After Jesus had gone head to head with the Devil in the wilderness, Matthew records, "Angels came and took care of him." With divine irony, Jesus experienced the psalmist's promise that Satan had twisted to tempt him. We receive the same promise in the Epistle of Peter.

> Be clearheaded. Keep alert. Your accuser, the devil, is on
> the prowl like a roaring lion, seeking someone to devour.
> Resist him, standing firm in the faith . . . After you have

12. Lewis, *Mere Christianity*, 126.

suffered for a little while, the God of all grace, the one who called you into his eternal glory in Christ Jesus, will himself restore, empower, strengthen, and establish you. (1 Pet 5:8–11)

Katherine Guerrero was preaching in the Homegrown North Carolina Women's Preaching Festival when she shared the story of her undocumented crossing of the wilderness at the US-Mexico border as a child. She remembered holding tightly to her mother's hand as they made their way in the darkness of the night. In spite of her fear, she bore witness to "the God she discovered in the dark, the God who traveled with her." Jerusha Neal described how it felt to be in the congregation and linked Katherine's story to the coming of Christ when she wrote, "Finally, a different undocumented crossing comes into view: the crossing of God from heaven to earth, born in moonlight, searching for a mother's hand."[13]

God is there with us in the wilderness. By the presence of the Holy Spirit, the wilderness can become the place we find the grace of God. Thomas Merton bore witness to that experience when he wrote:

> The soul one day begins to realize, in a manner completely unexpected and surprising, that in the darkness it has found the living God. It is overwhelmed with the sense that He is there and that His love is surrounding and absorbing it on all sides. In fact, He has been there all the time . . . Nothing else matters.[14]

On the other side of temptation, the wilderness becomes a place of clarity about what is in our head and heart and what matters most. It's a terrible place to lose our bearings, but it can also be the place where we find them. And that will make all the difference.

13. Neal, *Overshadowed Preacher*, 122–23.
14. Merton, *Inner Experience*, 87.

Questions for Reflection

How do you experience temptation?

What would it mean for you to choose the way of the Kingdom of God rather than the kingdoms of this world?

When have you seen or experienced the assurance of God's presence in times of temptation?

3

Preaching in Nazareth

Read: Luke 4:1–30, Matthew 13:53–58

The trip back home got off to a great start but turned into a disaster. Any preacher would be hard pressed to find a sermon that started out better and ended up worse than the one Jesus preached in Nazareth. How could a day that began so well end so badly? How did what happened in his hometown help Jesus find his bearings for the ministry ahead?

"Jesus went to Nazareth, where he had been raised."
(Luke 4:16)

Nazareth was a tiny, nondescript Jewish village not unlike Anatevka, the poor Jewish community in the Broadway musical *Fiddler on the Roof*. Nathanael was probably not the only outsider who wondered, "Can anything good come out of Nazareth?" (John 1:46 NRSV). It was the kind of place where nothing much ever happened but where everyone knew everything about everyone else.

Nazareth was Mary's hometown, the place where the angel Gabriel surprised her with the promise that she would bear a son and name him Jesus (Luke 1:26–30). Joseph received the equally surprising word that Mary's child was "conceived by the Holy Spirit" and that he was to name the child Jesus, "because he will save his people from their sins" (Matt 1:18–25). Nazareth was where they returned with their little boy after their escape to Egypt as immigrants seeking asylum from Herod's murderous jealousy and political insecurity. For the next thirty years, Nazareth was Jesus' hometown, the place where he had been raised.

I wonder what Jesus might have been feeling as he set his internal GPS to go back to his hometown.

I follow a Facebook group that shares memories of the small town where I grew up. Visiting that site reminds me of people, places, and events that defined my childhood and shaped my adolescence. Because Jesus was in every way like every one of us (Heb 4:15), he must have experienced some of the emotions we feel when we go back to the place where we grew up. For some people, there's no better place on earth. For others, it's the place they spend the rest of their lives trying to forget. For most of us, returning to those places conjures memories of joy and pain, hope and disappointment, gratitude and regret.

Jesus' return to Nazareth occurs later in Matthew (13:53–58) and Mark (6:1–6), but Luke placed it at the beginning of Jesus' ministry, immediately following his wrestling match with the Devil. Just as he was "led by the Spirit into the wilderness," he "returned in the power of the Spirit to Galilee." If the wilderness was the kind of place where Jesus might have lost his bearings, you might expect Nazareth to be the kind of place where he would find his bearings for the future.

The trip through Galilee got off to an impressive start with a star quality visit to Capernaum. Jesus "taught in their synagogues and was praised by everyone" (Luke 4:14). The crowds applauded, the popularity polls were in his favor, but as we will see in the rest of the story, premature praise can be disturbingly unpredictable.

Early in my ministry I learned through painful experience that the same people who give excessive affirmation at the beginning can quickly turn against a young pastor who doesn't live up to their expectations, does something they don't approve, makes stupid mistakes, or preaches a word they don't want to hear. Believing everything the applauding crowds say can provide Satan with a prime opportunity for temptation.

A fellow pastor was speaking to clergy colleagues in a training session on sexual ethics. He acknowledged that when he was "flying high" in the ministry, when things were going well and everyone seemed to be cheering, were times when he was most vulnerable to temptation because he was "too full of himself." Pastoral friends who tumbled into moral disaster were generally successful people who mistakenly believed that it could never happen to them.

Perhaps by placing the Nazareth story immediately after Jesus' crowd-pleasing journey through Galilee, Luke was suggesting that there was one more test for Jesus before beginning his ministry.

> "On the Sabbath he went to the synagogue
> as he normally did." (Luke 4:16)

Like life in Anatevka, life in Nazareth was bound together by Jewish ritual and tradition. *The New York Times* columnist David Brooks grew up in that kind of community in New York City. His feelings about the kosher rules "oscillated between ferocious resentment and profound respect." He "resented a practice that can descend into dry and pedantic legalism." At the same time, he respected how "Judaism has a ritual for every occasion." In his spiritual journey toward Christianity, Brooks found that "the first ramp is the ramp of ritual . . . collective enactments of the moral order and a sacred story."[1]

Keeping the sabbath was one of the essential rituals included in the *mitzvot,* the 613 commandments that God gave to the people of Israel. It was grounded in the way God blessed the seventh day of creation as a day of rest (Exod 20:8–11). The sabbath also came to embody the irrepressible hope for the fulfillment of God's redemption and the healing of creation. Like everyone else in Nazareth, Jesus went to the synagogue on the sabbath "as was his custom" (Luke 4:16 NRSV).

---

1. Brooks, *Second Mountain,* 225, 257.

I grew up with the same custom. As we were "sheltering in place" during the coronavirus crisis, I realized how deeply I missed the custom of being in church on Sunday morning. As a child I never had to decide what to do on Sunday; my parents made that decision for me before I was born. Our unwavering custom was to be in Sunday School (I have a string of perfect attendance pins to prove it!) and worship followed by the equally customary stop at Eddie Weidner's News Room (the only store open on Main Street on Sunday back then) to pick up *The Pittsburgh Press* on the way home where the equally customary aroma of roast beef with potatoes and carrots filled the house.

As was the custom for every Jewish male, Jesus would have worn the *tallit*, the rectangular, woolen shawl with strings or fringes called *tzitzit* on the four corners. Touching the *tzitzit* was a tactile way to "remember all the Lord's commands and do them" (Num 15:37–40). Early synagogue practice suggests that any adult male who could read could stand up, be recognized, and be given the opportunity to read the Scripture. So, Jesus stood, received the scroll, and unrolled it to Isaiah.

New Testament scholar Richard Hays says Luke is constantly inviting us to "read backwards" by seeing Old Testament events and characters that are "woven into the fabric of the story." While the primary action is center stage, "a screen at the back of the stage displays a kaleidoscopic series of . . . images from Israel's Scripture."[2] In this case, the image of Israel's greatest prophet hovered over the synagogue as Jesus read:

> The Lord God's spirit is upon me,
> because the Lord has anointed me.
> He has sent me
> to bring good news to the poor,
> to bind up the brokenhearted,
> to proclaim release for captives,
> and liberation for prisoners,
> to proclaim the year of the Lord's favor . . . (Isa 61:1–2)

2. Hays, *Reading Backwards*, 58–9.

The words must have been music in the ears of the people in the synagogue. Isaiah's vision awakened deep feelings for every faithful Israelite, something like the emotion many citizens of the United States experience when they read the Gettysburg Address or sing the "Battle Hymn of the Republic."

Jesus read from what scholars identify as Third Isaiah (Isa 56–66). It was addressed to people who had returned from exile and were rebuilding Jerusalem. Chapters 60–62 form the central core of this prophecy, beginning with the exuberant shout, "Arise! Shine! Your light has come; the Lord's glory has shone upon you." It is a hope-filled, joy-soaked vision of God's promised future when "the Lord will be an everlasting light for you, and your days of mourning will be ended" (Isa 60:1, 20).

The prophet declares, "The Spirit of the Lord is upon me because the Lord . . . has sent me to bring good news" (Isa 61:1). To "bring good news" refers to the messenger who comes in advance of the returning forces to announce victory over an enemy or liberation for people in bondage. The messenger is, therefore, "the bringer of joy"[3] who announces what God has already done and will do in the future.

We were discussing Jesus' sermon in the Nazareth synagogue in a men's group when one of the guys observed that all of the people mentioned in the passage from Isaiah are the disenfranchised: poor, blind, imprisoned, and oppressed. It led to the awareness that Isaiah's promise is good news for people who are marginalized because of economic condition, excluded because of race or sexual identity, rejected because of immigration status. The prophesy is joyful, liberating news for people who are lost, alone, and hopeless.

Isaiah's announcement of "the year of the Lord's favor" was a reminder of the "Jubilee Year" in Leviticus 25. It envisioned a time when debts were to be forgiven and debtors released from bondage. The land would be returned to families who had lost it through financial failure. The Jubilee called for "an equitable and widespread distribution of the land . . . to prevent the accumulation of ownership in the hands of a wealthy few." It also "aimed

---

3. Moltmann, *Way of Christ*, 95.

to restore social dignity . . . to families through maintaining or restoring their economic viability."[4] The jubilee was grounded in the Lord's declaration, "The land is mine; with me you are but aliens and tenants" (Lev 25:23 NRSV).

There is scholarly debate about the extent to which the Jubilee was fully practiced, but the ideal of liberation and socioeconomic justice was passed down in our history in the words inscribed on the Liberty Bell: "Proclaim liberty throughout all the land unto all the inhabitants thereof" (Lev 25:10 KJV).

It's interesting to notice what Jesus left out of Isaiah's prophesy. He stopped reading before Isaiah's announcement of "the day of vengeance of our God" (61:2 NRSV). The deletion makes clear that Jesus' agenda does not include revenge and violence. The good news Jesus proclaimed with his words and demonstrated with his life is a way out of our deadly addiction to the diabolical myth of redemptive violence. As we will see in the Sermon on the Mount, he reinterprets Scripture to call his followers away from the endless cycle of eye-for-an-eye revenge and into the way of redemptive reconciliation and transformative peace (Matt 5:38–48).

It's also important to observe that Isaiah's prophesy was not addressed to individuals, but to the nation as a whole. It was not primarily a vision of personalized piety or solitary spirituality, but a transformative call to participate in the fulfillment of God's promise of justice and liberation through social and economic practices in the community. In quoting Isaiah, Jesus declared that God's agenda is not only the transformation of individual lives, but the transformation of the social, cultural, economic, political, and religious systems in which we live.

I'm grateful for every way the Spirit of God alleviates the poverty of my spirit, binds up the brokenness in my life, releases me from my self-absorbed bondage, and opens my spiritually blind eyes. But we should not over-personalize this text. The good news Jesus proclaimed is not just personal; it's also social and political. It's not just private; it's also public. It's not just about me getting right

---

4. Freedman, *Anchor Dictionary*, 1029.

with God; it's also about God using me to get the economic and social systems of this world right with God's saving purpose.

As the "bringer of joy," Jesus announced God's victory not only over the personal demons in the human soul but over the "principalities and powers" (Eph 6:12 KJV) that keep poor people poor, that oppress people's freedom, that divide the community by race, class, or sexual orientation, and that are opposed to God's redemptive justice and liberating love. By claiming Isaiah's vision as his own, Jesus announced a victory that God has already won and that will be fulfilled at the end of time.

Questions for Reflection

Read Isaiah 60–61 aloud. How does Isaiah's announcement make you feel?

How does the prophetic vision impact your understanding of the social and economic issues of our time?

What might it mean for you to affirm, "The Spirit of the Lord is upon me"?

"Today, this scripture has been fulfilled." (Luke 4:21)

A thick silence permeated the synagogue as Jesus rolled up the scroll, handed it back to the assistant, and sat down. It was what rabbis did when they moved from reading Scripture to teaching or debating it. Luke says every eye "was fixed on him" in anticipation of what the hometown boy was going to say.

We had a similar experience when my twin brother and I were invited back to First United Methodist Church in Clarion, Pennsylvania, to celebrate the 100th anniversary of their church building. It's the church where we were baptized and confirmed, the congregation that patiently nurtured our adolescent faith and encouraged us to follow God's call into the ministry, the place where we returned to bury our parents. We had moved to other parts of the country, but they had heard about our ministries and wanted to see how those skinny boys had turned out. In that setting, no one expected preaching that offends or disrupts long-held assumptions. I suspect that assumption was true of folks in Nazareth, too.

Jesus began by declaring, "Today this scripture has been fulfilled in your hearing" (Luke 4:21 NRSV). He used the words of Isaiah to announce his mission and to set the course of his ministry. It was similar to a President declaring the agenda of the new administration at the Inauguration.

At first, the people heard this as good news. Luke says they were "raving about Jesus, so impressed were they by the gracious words flowing from his lips" (4:22). They had long hoped that Isaiah's prophecy would be fulfilled someday, somewhere, but Jesus claimed that the Kingdom, reign, and rule of God was becoming a present reality, right here, right now, in Nazareth!

I received an email from a faithful skeptic in the congregation who asked, "We pray, 'Your Kingdom come,' but in today's world of slick imagery and sophisticated marketing, how would we know the real thing vs. the fake or the pretender? How would we know the difference between Hollywood, Hucksters, and Heaven?" It's a good question. If our prayer for God's will to be done and God's Kingdom to come on earth were answered right here, right now, how would we recognize it? It's the question a skeptical John the Baptist sent to Jesus from Herod's prison. "Are you the one who is to come, or should we look for another?" Before he died, John needed to know how to separate the real thing from a fake. Jesus replied with words from Isaiah:

> Report to John what you hear and see. Those who were blind are able to see. Those who were crippled are walking. People with skin diseases are cleansed. Those who were deaf now hear. Those who were dead are raised up. The poor have good news proclaimed to them. Happy are those who don't stumble and fall because of me. (Matt 11:2–6, Isa 35:5–6, 61:1)

If the Kingdom of God is, in fact, becoming a reality here and now, what does it look like? The answer is that the Kingdom of God looks like Jesus. Watch what Jesus does. Listen to what Jesus says. Follow the way Jesus lives and dies. Experience the transformation Jesus brings in the lives of marginalized people who are bind, crippled, disease infected, deaf, and poor. In Jesus, you can see what it looks like for Isaiah's promise to be actualized in human life. This is what it looks like for God's Kingdom to come and God's will to be done on earth as it is in heaven. The real thing looks like the way Jesus fulfilled Isaiah's vision.

Back home in Nazareth, Jesus declared that the Kingdom comes through ordinary people in ordinary places like the people in the synagogue that day. It is not just for some distant future. It is God's redemptive rule and gracious reign becoming a reality in singularly insignificant, nondescript, out-of-the-way places like Nazareth.

I was among a group of seminary students who, in the aftermath of Woodstock, began one of the first Christian music festivals known as *Ichthus*. The Greek word translated "fish" was an early Christian acronym for *Jesus Christ, God's Son, Savior*. I remember hearing the African-American evangelist Tom Skinner tell that crowd of young people that praying for God's Kingdom to come on earth as it is in heaven means that if anyone wants to know what's going on in heaven, they ought to be able to look at us. His words have lingered in my memory across the years as a reminder that God's Kingdom, promised by Isaiah and present among us in Jesus, is intended to be a flesh-and-blood reality today through ordinary people like every one of us.

The hometown folks were impressed! Frankly, this would have been an excellent time for Jesus to quit preaching! But then a suspicious question percolated among the people in the synagogue.

"This is Joseph's son, isn't it?" (Luke 4:22)

It's one of most enigmatic questions in the New Testament. Everything depends on the tone in which it was asked. They might have been asking it with community pride, like the hometown folks who see one of their high school baseball players make the big leagues.

"Look how well he's doing. He's one of ours! He's Joe's boy!" But the same question turned in the opposite direction and the people were "repulsed by him" (Mark 6:2–3).

The folks in Nazareth had not forgotten the questionable timing of Jesus' birth. You can imagine self-righteous gossips in the back of the synagogue whispering to each other, "Isn't this Joseph's son?" "Ah, yes! He's the illegitimate one, Joseph's bastard son." They had heard peculiar stories about Jesus' birth in Bethlehem. They had received ominous reports of what Simeon and Anna predicted at Jesus' dedication (Luke 2:21–38). Some of them saw the way Jesus behaved in the Temple when he was twelve years old (Luke 2:41–50). These were stories Mary kept in her heart but refused to tell (Luke 2:51). They had kept a cagey eye on him across decades prior to that day when John baptized him in the Jordan and Jesus disappeared into the wilderness. And they had caught wind of the crowds that welcomed him in Capernaum.

Jesus overheard the backrow murmuring and responded, "Doubtless you will quote to me this proverb, 'Doctor, cure yourself!' And you will say, 'Do here also in your hometown the things that we have heard you did at Capernaum'" (Luke 4:23). That's when the wheels came off the sermonic wagon!

The faithful Jews in Nazareth didn't like those people in Capernaum. It was a largely Gentile, non-Jewish community. The hometown folks were deeply offended by the reports of what Jesus did there. To make matters worse, Jesus reminded them of two of their least favorite stories in Scripture.

> Truly I tell you, no prophet is accepted in the prophet's hometown. But the truth is, there were many widows in Israel in the time of Elijah, when the heaven was shut up three years and six months, and there was a severe famine over all the land; yet Elijah was sent to none of them except to a widow at Zarephath in Sidon. There were also many lepers in Israel in the time of the prophet Elisha, and none of them was cleansed except Naaman the Syrian. (Luke 4:24–27)

The hometown folks were deeply offended by those stories. There were plenty of hungry widows in Israel, so why did Elijah go over to non-Jewish Sidon to feed a Gentile widow (1 Kgs 17:8–15)? They remembered the shocking story about Elisha healing a pagan leper named Naaman the Syrian (2 Kgs 5:1–19). Why didn't Elijah and Elisha take care of their own people first?

Both stories ran against the grain of the religious, ethnic, and cultural exclusivity of their homogeneous community, but those were the stories Jesus used to describe what he was doing. He had the audacity to say that the way God sent Elijah to Sidon and the way God used Elisha to heal a Syrian was the same way the Spirit of the Lord was sending him beyond the boundaries of their narrow cultural identity with good news for the poor, release for the captives, recovery of sight for the blind, liberation for the oppressed, and to announce the Lord's all-inclusive love for people the folks in Nazareth assumed were shut out of God's concern.

Jesus knew the hometown crowd. He knew their xenophobic prejudice, their intolerance toward Gentiles, and their disdain for anyone who wasn't exactly the same as they were. He had grown up with their rigid legalism and crass insensitivity to marginalized, disenfranchised people. He applied the Scripture to their community the way a surgeon applies a scalpel to a cancerous tumor, knowing that it will cause pain, but also knowing that it is the only way to healing. It was a sermon that called for repentance and conversion. It necessitated a radical reorientation of their lives and a determined reversal to walk in a new direction.

Jesus put himself squarely in the line of the Old Testament prophets who reminded the covenant people that they had been blessed by God to be a blessing to the whole world. The blessing of God was not something to be held within the narrow confines of their tradition but to be shared with the least likely people. Throughout his ministry, Jesus reinterpreted Scripture in a way that contradicted the most tightly held prejudices of the people of Nazareth, just the way his parables continue to unhinge some of our most tightly held assumptions today. One of my seminary professors said that if we really want to hear what Jesus is saying, we should look for the place where he offends us.

As a homecoming sermon, it was a disaster! Luke reports that everyone was "filled with anger." The formerly impressed people in the synagogue "rose up and ran him out of town. They led him to the crest of the hill . . . so that they could throw him off the cliff" (Luke 4:28–30).

It's a disturbing warning for any preacher! Peter Gomes, now deceased, was the minister in the Memorial Church at Harvard University when he wrote, "It is very difficult to preach the gospel as Jesus did without giving offense, and the world has been filled with people perfectly capable of being offended."[5]

It's an equally disturbing story for every follower of Jesus. When we listen deeply to his words, their meaning will inevitably cut so deeply into our lives that our instinctive tendency for self-protection will lead us to reject them. There are, of course, parts of Scripture that comfort the afflicted. But the prophetic words of the Old Testament that became flesh in Jesus are just as clearly intended to afflict our comfortable, cozy complacency as they uncover the evil, sin, selfishness, and injustice within and around us.

It is possible to read the Bible in ways that protect us from the sharp scalpel of God's healing word.

We can say we believe the Bible, but impulsively reject the words that push against the grain of our political, ideological, economic, national, or social traditions.

We can claim to take the Bible literally but refuse to take Jesus seriously when it comes to matters of justice, violence, poverty, and peacemaking.

We can pray for God's kingdom to come and God's will to be done on earth, while restricting that prayer to a spiritual stratosphere, safely removed from the messy stuff of our lives, our nation, and our world.

Or we can hear the prophetic word as God's sometimes painful but always liberating, life-giving word for us and for the whole world.

5. Gomes, *Scandalous Gospel*, 20.

The sermon Jesus delivered in Nazareth became a living, penetrating word for me as I worked on this book. I asked several African-American colleagues to read the first draft with a sensitive eye to the way I described the crisis of racial reckoning in our nation and our church. One of them encouraged me to write in a way that might awaken my predominately white readership to the authentic pain Black people experience, to the ways white Christians continue to be complicit through silence and indifference in supporting rather than dismantling racist systems in society and within the church, and to healthy guilt or shame that leads to empathy and action that helps heal, reconcile, and transform the world into God's "beloved community."

This same friend cared enough about my own journey to challenge me not to stand at a distance as an objective observer, but to engage more deeply with the harm and suffering incurred on people of color by my ancestors so as to own the way I've benefited from that pain, including ways I may have failed to do all that I might have done to address these critical issues across the years of my ministry.

I confess that my first response was defensive. After all, I've been preaching about and engaging with these issues for forty years! But rather than reject that message the way the people in Nazareth rejected the same message from Jesus, I've been living more prayerfully with it, listening more deeply to it, acknowledging more fully the truth of it, and searching for the way I can become more directly engaged in God's work of transformation and reconciliation, even daring to pray that this book might be a small contribution to that healing. I'm not yet where I am called to be, but it's been another necessary step in walking the way Jesus walked in the way that he walked it.

Questions for Reflection

How have you seen the Kingdom of God becoming a reality?

When has a passage of Scripture offended you? Why?

What difference does Jesus' description of the Kingdom make in your life?

"He passed through the crowd and went on his way."
(Luke 4:30)

Jesus is consistently identified as "Jesus of Nazareth" in the Gospels and the Book of Acts. It was the name by which Pilate identified Jesus when he was nailed to the cross (John 19:19). But Jesus never went home again. Matthew records, "He left Nazareth and settled in Capernaum" (Matt 4:13). From there, he became an itinerate rabbi who had "no place to lay his head" (Luke 9:58) as he "traveled through the cities and villages, preaching and proclaiming the good news of God's kingdom" (Luke 8:1).

I tried to feel what Jesus might have felt as he left the place where he grew up. He was not the person the hometown folks expected or wanted him to be. To them, he was still Joseph's bastard son. Through his baptism and his testing in the wilderness, he had become the "bringer of joy" anointed by the Spirit to bring the good news of God's Kingdom, but he had been soundly and painfully rejected by the very people who had taught him to read the Scriptures. The prophetic vision that had become "an intense fire in [his] heart" (Jer 20:9) had ignited fires of resentment and opposition in the hearts of his childhood friends and neighbors.

I tried to imagine what Mary and Joseph felt as they watched him walk away that day. It must have been similar to the way John Lewis's parents watched their son leave their tiny, segregated community to enter seminary and be trained in Jesus' way of nonviolence. Jon Meacham writes, "They knew . . . at the beginning of their son's journey, that he was taking a difference path." Lewis remembered "the mixture of fear and concern they both felt as they watched me walk out into the world as a young man and join a movement aimed at turning the world they knew upside down."[6]

I wondered if this moment in the synagogue was Mary's first experience of the sword that Simeon predicted would pierce her

6. Meacham, *Truth Is Marching*, 43.

heart (Luke 2:35). Did Joseph feel some pang of regret that he "did just as an angel from God commanded him" (Matt 1:24)? What combination of rejection and pity did they face from their neighbors and friends because of what their son had said and become?

Luke isn't the least bit interested in answering those questions. He simply says that Jesus "went on his way." Jesus was no more intimidated by the rejection in Nazareth than he was impressed by the praise in Capernaum. He had found his bearings and went on his way with a calm, steady clarity in who God had declared him to be and what God was calling him to do. One thing is clear: he never forgot the things he learned in Nazareth. The words of Scripture he heard, read, and memorized in his childhood continued to be the internal compass that would guide him along the way that would ultimately lead to the cross.

When I left the place where I grew up, my journey led to Florida. A few years later, I returned to visit my father who was dying with cancer. At the end of a visit that was much more positive than Jesus' return to Nazareth, I took a commuter flight to Pittsburgh to catch my flight home. I watched out the window as the low-flying plane followed familiar roads through the rolling hills and small towns where four generations of my family had lived, died, and were buried. I felt the presence of the ghosts of people I had left behind in a place where I would never live again. They were the people who led me to Christ and nurtured me as his follower. I heard them saying, "You are free to go, but don't forget us." There would be other visits for reunions, weddings, and funerals, but in an oddly unemotional but deeply clarifying way, in that moment I felt free to "leave the past behind and reach out to whatever was ahead" (Phil 3:14 AP). I knew I had found my bearings to the place I expected to serve in ministry for the rest of my life.

I remember a seminary friend who was preparing to go back home to Northern Ireland during some of the worst days of the conflict remembered as "the Troubles." Above his study desk, he had posted his own version of a prayer attributed to David Livingston, the early missionary to Africa:

Send me anywhere, only go with me.

Lay any burden upon me, only sustain me.

Break any tie except the tie that binds me to You.

Whatever he might have felt, Jesus left Nazareth with the clarity of his calling. He knew the way he would follow. In spite of rejection and risk, his mission and his message were unmistakably and irrevocably clear. It was time for him to move on.

Questions for Reflection

When have you walked away from your past to follow some new opportunity or calling?

What do you imagine Jesus, Mary, and Joseph were feeling as Jesus left Nazareth?

Is there something you need to leave behind if you are to continue walking with Jesus?

4

Teaching on the Mountain

Read: Matthew 5:1–48

M ountains are sometimes more challenging to climb than we expected, but they often turn out to be more than worth the effort.

The skies were clear over Cape Town when we arrived in South Africa. Greg, our fellow Methodist pastor and host, suggested we hike up Lion's Head, which rises 2,195 feet between Table Mountain and Signal Hill. It looked intimidating, but Greg, a competitive athlete who had hiked the mountain many times, promised it would help us to get our bearings looking out over one of the world's most beautiful cities.

Greg led the way with his toddler daughter in his backpack and his small dog at his side. We could have chosen the "Spiral Route" that winds around the mountain with a more gradual incline, but trusting our leader, we took the "Chains Route." The "Must Read" sign at the beginning of the trail warns, "You could be exposed to rugged terrain . . . By entering this area you accept the inherent risk."

The paved walkway soon turned into well-worn gravel until it became a dirt footpath. When it led upward using chain ladders and steel handholds bolted to the rocks, I considered letting my team members, all of whom were at least ten years younger than I, go on without me! But exhausted and slightly out of breath, we reached the wind-swept summit and found our bearings as we looked out over the city and toward the "Twelve Apostles," the rugged peaks that make their silent march to the Atlantic coastline.

Had I known how challenging the climb would become, I might have chosen the easier path, but I'm grateful we trusted our leader and took the way less traveled. It made all the difference and became a high point (literally and figuratively) of the visit.

Jesus gathered his followers on a very different mountain where he painted the word picture of a wide, easy way that many people follow. By contrast, he said the way "that leads to life is narrow and the road difficult, so few people find it" (Matt 7:13–14). There are inherent risks and often rugged terrain when we make our way by walking the way Jesus lays out for us in the Sermon on the Mount, but it's more than worth the effort. It is, in fact, the way that leads to life!

> "He went up a mountain. He sat down and his disciples
> came to him." (Matt 5:1)

The place of the teaching and the posture of the teacher are deeply rooted in the Hebrew Scriptures. Written primarily for a Jewish audience, Matthew's Gospel placed Jesus "on a mountain" where he "sat down." In Luke's Gospel, written for a largely Gentile audience, Jesus "came down from the mountain . . . and stood on a large area of level ground" (Luke 6:17).

Mountains are decisive places for Matthew. They are places where people experience God's presence and find their bearings for the way ahead (Matt 4:8, 14:23,15:29, 17:1, 24:3 28:16). In this case, the mountain conjures up the memory of Mt. Sinai where Moses received the Law that shaped the way of life for the Hebrew people (Exod 19–20).

If Lion's Head looked intimidating to me, it was no comparison to the "thunder, lightning, and a thick cloud on the mountain" at Sinai. No wonder "all the people shook with fear." But whereas God came down on Mt. Sinai with "the smoke of a hot furnace, while the whole mountain shook violently" (Exod

19:16–18), Matthew's mountainside is peaceful and serene. Instead of shaking with fear, the disciples and we with them are drawn to Jesus out of an experience of love, a promise of healing, and a hope for liberation.

The preamble to the Sermon (Matt 4:23–5:1) finds Jesus teaching in the synagogues, announcing "the good news of the kingdom," and healing "every disease and sickness among the people" (Matt 4:23). Everything Jesus says and does becomes the living demonstration of the Kingdom of God that is not yet fully come but is fully present in Jesus. Roman Catholic theologian Hans Küng declared, "The Kingdom of God is creation healed."[1]

Matthew's preamble leads us to the mountain where God speaks, the teacher through whom God's word is delivered, the disciples whose lives are to be formed by these words, and the Kingdom, God's not-yet-fulfilled but fully-present reign in Jesus. When Jesus' words are lifted out of this context to be passed on like advice from Benjamin Franklin's *Poor Richard's Almanac,* they become bits of inspirational guidance that look fine on motivational posters but are nearly impossible to achieve.

Philip Yancy reported the way Virginia Stem Owens discovered the challenge of the Sermon on the Mount when she assigned it to students in her composition class at Texas A&M University. Most of the students had never read it before. One of them responded, "It made me feel like I had to be perfect and no one is." Another reacted, "The things asked in this sermon are absurd." Owens described their comments as "a pristine response to the gospel, unfiltered through a two-millennia cultural haze."[2]

The students got it right! The Sermon on the Mount is downright absurd unless it is describing a way of living that is consistent with and a preview of the Kingdom of God: the redemptive will, saving purpose, and healing love of God at work in human experience and history. It defines the way for people who "desire first and foremost God's kingdom and God's righteousness"

---

1. Küng, *On Being a Christian,* 231.

2. Yancey, *Jesus I Never Knew,* 130.

(Matt 6:33). It's the way we become active participants in God's healing and transformation of the world.

How do people find their way into this Kingdom-shaped life? Sometimes we believe our way into a new way of behaving while other times we behave our way into a new way of believing.

The Sermon on the Mount has very little to say about *what* Jesus' disciples believe. It's primarily about *how* they behave. Jesus warns, "Not everybody who says to me, 'Lord, Lord,' will get into the kingdom of heaven. Only those who *do* the will of my Father." He promises that everyone who "hears these words of mine and *puts them into practice* is like the builder who built a house on bedrock" (Matt 7:21, 24; emphasis mine).

Jesus' teachings may reflect what David Brooks experienced as a Jewish assumption that "behavior change precedes and causes internal change."[3] John Wesley learned that lesson in a time when he was "clearly convinced of unbelief, of the want of that faith whereby alone we are saved." He asked Peter Bohler, his spiritual mentor and guide, if he should stop preaching faith because he didn't have it himself. Bohler replied, "By no means. Preach faith till you have it; and then, because you have it, you will preach faith."[4]

Whether we find our bearings through belief or behavior, the Sermon on the Mount pinpoints the summit toward which Jesus leads us by reiterating a disturbing imperative from the Old Testament: "You must be perfect before the Lord your God" (Deut 18:13).

Questions for Reflection

How does the preamble (Matt 4:23–5:1) prepare you to hear the Sermon on the Mount?

How have you experienced the connection between belief and behavior?

What do you feel when you read the word "perfect"?

3. Brooks, *Second Mountain*, 225.
4. Wesley, *Journal*, 32.

"Be perfect, therefore, as your heavenly Father is perfect." (Matt 5:48 NRSV)

Our hike up Lion's Head confirmed that our vantage point, the
position from which we saw the mountain, had a direct impact
on how we anticipated the journey ahead. Similarly, how people
dealt with the COVID-19 crisis largely depended on their vantage
point, their life experience, and the internal compass of the values
and ideals that motivated their behavior. To a large extent, how
they behaved in the present depended on their vision of the end or
goal toward which they were going in the future.

I invite you to join me in viewing the Sermon on the Mount
from the vantage point of Jesus' call to "be perfect as your
heavenly Father is perfect" (Matt 5:48 NRSV). E. Stanley Jones
declared this "astonishing statement" to be "the central ideal"
around which the entire Sermon "revolves as on a pivot."[5] When
we see the Sermon from this vantage point, Jesus' words become
the end or goal toward which we are walking as we walk the way
Jesus walked in the way that he walked it.

Fifty years after my ordination, I continue to be challenged by
John Wesley's historic questions every year when the bishop asks
them of new candidates for ordination at our Annual Conference.

Are you going on to perfection?

Do you expect to be made perfect in love in this life?

Are you earnestly striving after it?[6]

Wesley's questions are not, however, for ordained people alone;
they set our bearings on the summit to which Jesus is leading every
disciple. Paul reiterated this goal when he told the demonstrably
imperfect folks in Corinth, "This is what we pray for, that you may
become perfect" (1 Cor 13:9 NRSV).

If "perfection" is the end or goal of our discipleship, what
kind of perfection are we seeking?

---

5. Jones, *Christ of the Mount*, 36.

6. Franklyn, *Book of Worship*, 720.

In our culture, the word "perfect" conjures up images of Olympic athletes striving for a "perfect 10" in their events. As a young man, that's what Benjamin Franklin attempted to achieve. He called it "moral perfection" and set twelve "virtues" as his goal. Looking back as an older man, however, he confessed that mastering the virtues was much more difficult than he imagined.

Franklin was not mistaken in setting measurable goals for his behavior. John Wesley taught the early Methodists to measure their daily progress in holiness by evaluating their lives based on specific spiritual disciplines and personal behaviors. But Franklin's self-made and largely self-serving perfection is not the end that Jesus' followers seek.

The New Testament Greek adjective *teleios* describes that which is complete, whole, full grown, or mature. It's a root for the word "telescope," the tool that brings something far beyond us closer to us. The Hebrew word Jesus would have heard in the Nazareth synagogue was *tamim*. It comes from Israel's worship ritual in which only whole or unblemished animals could be offered to God. Applied to human behavior, it meant being completely loyal to God as embodied through whole-hearted obedience to the Law. Jesus may have recalled the command to be "perfect" from Moses' instruction for the priests not to be attracted to the gods or pagan practices of the people around them (Deut 18:9–14).

Jesus telescopes the entire biblical meaning of "perfection" into his command, "Therefore, just as your heavenly Father is complete in showing love to everyone, so also you must be complete" (Matt 5:48).

For followers of Jesus, "perfection" is the completion of the command to love God and to love others. It is the love of God that became flesh in Jesus becoming flesh in us, enabling us to love even our enemies with the universal love that causes the sun to shine and the rain to fall equally on the righteous and the unrighteous. It is not love as an emotion but love as intentionally chosen behavior. It's not a love generated by our own power, but a life-long process by which the Holy Spirit is relentlessly at work to complete God's loving purpose in and through our lives and in the whole creation.

The author of the first epistle of John must have had these words from Jesus in mind in writing:

> This is love: it is not that we loved God but that he loved us and sent his Son as the sacrifice that deals with our sins. Dear friends, if God loved us this way, we also ought to love each other . . . If we love each other, God remains in us and his love is made *perfect* in us. God is love, and those who remain in love remain in God and God remains in them. This is how love has been *perfected* in us . . . There is no fear in love, but *perfect* love drives out fear, because fear expects punishment. The person who is afraid has not been made *perfect* in love. (1 John 4:10–18; emphasis mine)

In *A Disciple's Heart,* we defined Christian perfection ("sanctification") as "God's way of love being worked out in human relationships . . . the goal toward which we are constantly moving . . . the relentless hope or heartfelt desire that persistently draws us toward something that is always beyond us." We also pointed out, "Christian perfection is not only about the transformation of the individual heart. It is also about the way people with transformed hearts participate in God's transformation of the world."[7]

For John Wesley, the goal of our discipleship is being made perfect in love. In his *Plain Account of Christian Perfection,* Wesley wrote, "The one perfect good shall be your one ultimate end." He called it the "one design" we "pursue to the end of time . . . In every step you take, be this the glorious point that terminates your view. Let every affection, and thought and word, and action, be subordinate to this."[8] Charles Wesley set the desire to music:

> Fill my heart with active love
>
> Emulating thee above.
>
> Love immense, and unconfined,
>
> Love to all of humankind.
>
> Love, which wills that all should live,

7. Harnish, *Disciple's Heart*, 19, 28, 108.
8. Wesley, "Plain Account," para. 7.

Love, which all to all would give,

Love, that over all prevails,

Love, that never, never fails.[9]

Christian perfection is not achieving moral perfection by human sweat and hard labor. Nor does it impose an insurmountable burden of guilt when we fall short of the goal. It is the life we see in Jesus becoming a reality in us. It is the summit toward which our discipleship is leading us.

I've never improved on the description of Christian perfection I learned from a wise farmer in the small, country church I served. When I asked, "How are you doing today?" he replied, "Well, Preacher, I'm not the man I used to be, and I'm not yet the man I'd like to be, but by God's grace I'm more the man God wants me to be than I've ever been before." He was going on to perfection!

Questions for Reflection

Are you "going on to perfection"?

Do you desire to be made complete in God's love in this life?

How are you earnestly striving after it?

"You have heard . . . but I say to you . . ." (Matt 5:17–48)

So, what does "being made perfect in love" look like in the messy, complex stuff of human behavior?

No one was better at achieving legalistic perfection than the Pharisees. It was their full-time job. The disciples must have gasped with surprise when Jesus declared, "Unless your righteousness is greater than the righteousness of the legal experts and the Pharisees, you will never enter the kingdom of heaven" (Matt 5:20).

We gasp, too! The "you-have-heard-but-I-say-to-you" assertions move the Old Testament laws beyond the way of legalism to

9. *United Methodist Hymnal*, no. 92.

the way of love. They describe the goal for imperfect people who are being made perfect in love.

We've heard that we should not murder (Exod 20:13), but Jesus goes beneath all our acts of violence to deal with the anger, hostility, and old-fashioned meanness that the coalescing crises of 2020 so ruthlessly exposed beneath the surface of our culture. The way of love leads toward radical reconciliation that breaks through the increasing alienation in our dangerously polarized political culture and the vicious racism that continues to infect our relationships.

We've heard that we should not commit adultery (Exod 20:14, Deut 5:18), but Jesus goes behind specific acts of sexual infidelity to the loveless desire to use another person for our own selfish pleasure. He challenges us to confront the misogyny, sexual abuse, and predatory behavior that has been uncovered by the Me Too Movement. In contrast, Jesus set the goal of a sexual ethic defined by trust and mutual respect.

We've heard that marriage is a contractual arrangement that can be undone in court (Deut 24:1), but Jesus goes beyond the contract to relationships that become a human expression of the covenant faithfulness of God. The way of love leads toward a radically unique commitment that can only be broken when unrepairable damage has been done and reconciliation becomes impossible.

We've heard that we should not "deceive nor lie to each other . . . not swear falsely" (Lev 19:11–12), but in a time when reality had become inundated in a flood of disinformation, the way of love demands a life of absolute integrity in which there is no room for "alternative facts" or "fake news." One Facebook post advised, "If you've got Jesus in your profile, don't be nasty on your timeline."

We've heard that we can practice even-handed revenge (Lev 24:20), but being made perfect in love shatters the obstinate myth of redemptive violence. We are called to Jesus' redemptive way of non-violence demonstrated by Martin Luther King Jr., Desmond Tutu, and John Lewis.

We've heard from the culture around us that we should love the people who like and are like us while hating those who dislike and are unlike us. But being made perfect in love calls us to include even the people we consider to be enemies within the circle of the commandment to love our neighbor as ourselves (Lev 19:18; Matthew 7:12).

The way of perfection is rooted in nothing less than the love that defines who God is and who we are as God's children, culminating in the command, "Just as God is complete in showing love to everyone, so also you must be complete."

Like the warning that by hiking Lion's Head we could be "exposed to rugged terrain," the way Jesus leads us is not easy stuff! The rugged truth is that Jesus' words run directly against the grain of some of the most deeply held assumptions of our lives and contradict some of the fundamental values of our culture. It's no surprise that we try to scuttle these words off into a corner of personal piety that never confronts the economic and social injustice of our day.

And yet, the disturbing truth is that Jesus actually expects his followers to behave this way! This is what it looks like to make our way by walking the way Jesus walked, in the way he walked it. His words force us to ask what kind of change needs to happen within us to enable us to practice a righteousness that is beyond the law.

As I was working on this chapter, I heard a helpful description of the difference between "incremental" and "transformational" change. Incremental change begins with what we already have, our basic assumptions and values. It works to improve the way we already function. Transformational change involves a radical reorientation of the assumptions and values by which we live, thereby resulting in fundamentally new ways of behaving.

If we only hear the Sermon on the Mount as a call to incremental change, it looks like an impossible hill to climb. But if we hear Jesus describing a transformational change it becomes an invitation to go beneath, behind and beyond the law to discover a thoroughly different way of living that fulfills the Lord's promise to Jeremiah, "I will put my law within them, and I will write it on their hearts" (Jer 31:33 NRSV).

The Sermon on the Mount is not a partial improvement of our way of behaving but a complete (*teleios*) reorientation of our way of being.

It's not righteousness defined by obligatory obedience to an impossible ethic but a right-related-ness with God in which the Spirit of God transforms the way we think and live.

It doesn't reject the Law, but fills the Law to overflowing with new life, love, and power.

It doesn't deny or try to escape the crises of the world around us but energizes our participation in the transformation of them.

It's not a way of life we achieve or accomplish on our own, but a way of loving that God does within, in, and through us and in community with others.

Jesus is not offering homespun bits of advice for more successful living but is lifting a vision of the end or goal of our discipleship. He is helping us find our bearings in a life-long pilgrimage of transformation along the way that leads to being made perfect in love.

Questions for Reflection

How do you understand the connection between Jesus' words and the Old Testament laws?

How do you experience the difference between incremental and transformational change?

Which "you-have-heard-but-I-say" statement is most troubling to you?

"If you want to be complete . . ." (Matt 19:21)

The word "perfect" (*teleios*) shows up again in Matthew's story of a rich man who asked Jesus, "What good thing must I do to have eternal life?" When Jesus asked about his obedience to the Law, he responded, "I've kept all these. What am I still missing?" Jesus challenged him to take a step beyond the law. "If you want to be complete (*teleios*), go sell what you own, and give the money to the poor. Then you will have treasure in heaven. And come follow me" (Matt 19:16–22). Jesus called for a transformational change in both his belief and his behavior. There is a soul-searching, silent pause as we wait to see what he will do.

Imagining the rich man in that crucial moment of decision, my memory meandered back to the Methodist camp meeting that played a formative role in my teenage spiritual development. At the conclusion of every service, we would be implored to come to the altar rail for prayer. I remembered singing:

> All to Jesus I surrender;
>
> all to him I freely give;
>
> I will ever love and trust him,
>
> in his presence daily live.
>
> I surrender all,
>
> I surrender all,
>
> all to Thee my blessed Savior,
>
> I surrender all.[10]

I'm not at all sure what the word *all* meant to me back then, but I know that my responses to those altar calls were beginning steps toward a life-long process of being made perfect in love. Across the years, the word *surrender* has come to mean releasing or letting go of specific prejudices, assumptions, actions, or patterns of behavior so that the way I live can be reoriented toward the way of Jesus. In themselves, many of those choices may have seemed insignificant, but each crisis became an opportunity to surrender another part of who I am, what I do, and what I value so that the Kingdom of God that was perfectly present in Jesus might become a more complete reality in my very imperfect life. It means continually surrendering all I know about myself to all that I know about Jesus in order to know myself and know him more deeply and follow him more completely.

10. Young, *United Methodist Hymnal*, 354.

Jesus knew that, for the rich man, going on toward perfection meant surrendering control of his wealth so that it could be used in ways that were consistent with the priorities of the Kingdom of God. The rich man may have come in search of incremental improvement, but Jesus called him to a transformational change in his relationship with his money. Walking with Jesus called for a complete reordering of his economic priorities that would result in a radically new level of generosity. The same thing happened for Zacchaeus when he climbed down from his tree, went home with Jesus, and found salvation from his greed by practicing economic justice for the people he had been cheating (Matt 19:1–9).

For followers of Jesus, the massive economic inequalities of our time call for a transformational change in our economic and social values that will result in equally profound changes in the way we invest and use our money, the economic and social policies we endorse, and the candidates for whom we vote. Praying "I surrender all" breaks us free from the wide-spread assumption that what I have is mine to do with as I choose, leading to the higher awareness that it's all God's, entrusted into our hands to use in ways that fulfill God's purpose.

Returning to the Gospel story, we watch in silence to see what the rich man will do. With a sigh and a drooping head, "He went away saddened, because he had many possessions." Jesus was evidently saddened, too. He acknowledged that it's not easy for rich people to make this kind of surrender, an observation that is undeniably confirmed in our contemporary culture. But he also promised, "All things are possible for God" (Matt 19:26).

E. Stanley Jones, writing out of his life-long ministry in India, said that Jesus' words in the Sermon on the Mount appear "as lofty as the Himalayan peaks—and as impossible. But put the warm touch of [Jesus'] reinvigorating fellowship into it, and anything—everything becomes possible."[11]

11. Jones, *Christ of the Mount*, 34.

Question for Reflection

How does the story of the rich man make you feel?

When have you experienced a challenge like this?

What are you being called to surrender to be more complete in your discipleship?

"Every good tree produces good fruit." (Matt 7:17)

What does the Sermon on the Mount do with, in, and through us? What kind of "good fruit" does it produce?

First, the Sermon on the Mount points us toward the summit as Jesus defines the perfect goal for imperfect disciples who are on the way to perfection.

While asking Wesley's historic questions, one bishop added, "If you aren't going on to toward perfection, where do you think you *are* going?" Without a clear vision of the end we seek, we can easily settle for lesser things or give up when we confront the inherent risks and rugged terrain along the way less traveled. But even when we fall short of their fulfillment, Jesus' words keep the summit clearly in view. It's what poet Robert Browning had in mind when he asked, "A man's reach should exceed his grasp, / Or what's a heaven for?"[12]

Second, the Sermon on the Mount forms what Jürgen Moltmann called a "contrast community" that "offers a viable alternative to [our] deadly vicious circle."[13] This is not a solo journey. We make our way in a "contrast community" with other disciples whose life together is a radical alternative to the values of the culture around them. It becomes the community in which we are held accountable for our progress and find support and encouragement along the way.

I would not have reached the summit of Lion's Head on my own. I needed a guide I could trust to know the way and a company

12. Browning, "Andrea del Sarto."
13. Moltmann, *Way of Jesus*, 125.

of friends to keep me going when I might have quit. As an imperfect follower of Jesus, when I'm tempted to compromise Jesus' ideals and settle for something less than "the high calling of God" (Phil 3:14 KJV), I need a "contrast community" to guide, challenge, encourage, and hold me accountable. None of us can make the journey alone. The good news is that we don't have to!

Third, the Sermon on the Mount calls us to action. Jesus warned that "only those who *do* the will of my Father" will enter the Kingdom (Matt 7:21; emphasis mine). Jesus expects us to participate in the coming of God's Kingdom by acting as if the Kingdom of God is already here . . . because it is!

Politicians who gathered for the 2020 National Prayer Breakfast were surprised when business professor Arthur Brooks applied Jesus' command to love our enemies to the political polarization in our nation. He challenged deeply divided political adversaries, "Ask God to give you the strength to do this hard thing, to go against your human nature, to follow Jesus' teaching . . . Sometimes, when it's just too hard, ask God to help you fake it."[14]

Fourth, the Sermon on the Mount promises that by God's grace we will be blessed and by God's power we will become a blessing to the world.

The bold, present tense, exclamatory affirmations of the Beatitudes (Matt 5:1–12) at the beginning of the sermon shock us by turning our cultural assumptions right-side up while turning them upside down. They affirm the end or goal of living the life to which Jesus calls us. He forcefully repeats the first word of the first Psalm, "Blessed is the [one] who . . ." (Ps 1:1 KJV). The Hebrew, *ashre*, appears more than twenty times in the Psalms to announce the true happiness and deep contentment of the God-centered life.

Matthew uses the Greek word *makarioi* to celebrate the astounding joy of those who are supremely blessed, extremely fortunate, or well off. It's the joy that moves far beyond giddy happiness because it flows from the transformative presence of God. The "blessed" life is not dependent on immediate circumstances or external success but is deeply rooted in God's promise

14. See "Arthur Brooks at National Prayer Breakfast."

to Abraham that he would be blessed and become a blessing to the world (Gen 12:2).

In the end, Jesus said that his disciples will not be known primarily by what they say they believe, but by the way they behave. They will be recognized by the fruit their lives produce, which Paul would later identify as the fruits of the Holy Spirit: "love, joy, peace, patience, kindness, goodness, faithfulness, gentleness, and self-control" (Gal 5:22–23).

The first draft of this chapter was nearing completion in the summer of our discontent when Representative John Lewis died. Looking back across the way Lewis joined the Freedom Riders who faced beatings, fire bombing, and possible death on bus rides into the deep South, the way he marched fearlessly across the Edmund Pettus bridge on Bloody Sunday, and the way he gave himself in consistently courageous leadership for equality and justice in Congress, we can see the way he demonstrated what it looks like to be strangely blessed by God in order to be a blessing to others. He put into practice the way of love to which Jesus calls every disciple.

The morning after Lewis died, historian and Lewis's biographer, Jon Meacham, called Lewis "a genuine saint . . . A human being willing to suffer and die for his understanding of the gospel and how that gospel found expression in the United States of America of the twentieth and twenty-first centuries." He summarized Lewis's life by saying, "He was about the Beatitudes . . . For him love was not an ideal but love was a reality . . . He was in the streets of America . . . because of Jesus of Nazareth."[15]

In his biography of Lewis, Meacham called Lewis "a prophet of the mountaintop . . . pointing toward the perfect."[16] John Lewis showed us that it may be a long way to the summit, along the way we will be exposed to rugged terrain, but the way to which Jesus calls us is, in fact, the narrow way that leads to life!

Let's give the final word to C. S. Lewis, who wrote that Jesus' command to be perfect is not "idealistic gas. Nor is it a command to do the impossible. He is going to make us into creatures

15. Meacham, "Historian Jon Meacham remembers Rep. John Lewis."

16. Meacham, *Truth Is Marching*, 8.

that can obey that command . . . The process will be long and in parts very painful; but that is what we are in for. Nothing less. He meant what he said."[17]

Question for Reflection

When have you seen the Sermon on the Mount becoming a reality in another person's life?

How do the beatitudes challenge your assumptions about what it means to be "blessed"?

What is your next step along the way toward the summit? Why would you settle for anything less?

17. Lewis, *Mere Christianity*, 176.

5

Dying at Golgotha

Read: Matthew 27:45–56, Mark 15:22–42,
Luke 23:33–49, John 19:16–30

When I completed the previous chapter, I told a friend, "Now, it's on to Golgotha." It always is. If we find our bearings by following Jesus, our spiritual GPS always leads to a rugged, skull-shaped hill on the outskirts of Jerusalem called Golgotha.

> "He went out to a place called Skull Place (in Aramaic, Gol-
> gotha). That's where they crucified him." (John 19:17–18)

Geographically, finding our bearings is easy enough. Tour guides can direct us to the probable place where subversives, terrorists, and anyone who dared to resist Roman power or question Roman authority were hung out to die in the most grotesque and gruesome form of capital punishment ever devised.

The Gospels, however, were not written to locate the "Skull Place" on a tourist's map of the Holy Land, but to lead us into the dark terrain of our own souls. The point is not to view Golgotha from a safe distance as an objective observer of a historical event, but to make our way as broken people in a broken world to that place where we fall in humility before the broken body of Jesus on the cross. When we hear the question, "Were you there when they crucified my Lord?" something deep within us cries out, "I am there!" In a way that is deeper than cognitive knowledge, we are confronted with the depth of human injustice, suffering, and sin. And there, when Jesus dies in the darkness at midday, we experience "the awful grace of God."

In the same way that Jesus recalled words from Scripture that were rooted deep within him in crucial moments in his life, Robert F. Kennedy recalled words from the Greek poet Aeschylus on that dark night he announced the assassination of Martin Luther King Jr. to an African-American audience in Indianapolis.

> Even in our sleep, pain which cannot forget
>
> falls drop by drop upon the heart,
>
> until, in our own despair,
>
> against our will,
>
> comes wisdom
>
> through the awful grace of God.[1]

At the cross, the awful, awesome and amazing grace of God "falls drop by drop upon the heart" as we realize that the sins that nailed Jesus to the cross were and continue to be the sins in our personal lives and the systemic evils that do our sinning for us. They are the sins that continue to nail innocent people to a cross today. And at the cross, we stand in awe as we discover that we can be redeemed through the unearned, undeserved, immeasurable forgiveness and grace of God.

I was guided to Golgotha during the racial crises of 2020 by the words of African-American theologian James H. Cone. His book *The Cross and the Lynching Tree* opened my eyes to the direct link between Jesus' crucifixion and lynching in America. He wrote that when African Americans sang about "the blood," they were:

> ... wrestling not only with the blood of the crucified carpenter from Nazareth but also with the blood of raped and castrated black bodies in America—innocent, often nameless, burning and hanging bodies, images of hurt

1. Kennedy, "Remarks."

so deep that only God's "amazing grace" could offer con-
solation . . . They felt something redemptive about Jesus'
cross . . . because "Calvary," in a mysterious way they
could not explain, was their redemption from the terror
of the lynching tree.[2]

After reading an early draft of this chapter, a young, faithful, African-American businessman and community leader confirmed
Cone's insight when he responded, "As a young black man I have
drawn the same parallels between the crucifixion and lynching
for years. Unprompted and unlearned, the symbolism is simply
embedded into my psyche."

Dr. Cone raised a disturbing question when he asked, "Can
one really understand the theological meaning of Jesus on a Roman cross without seeing him first through the image of blacks
on the lynching tree?"[3] That question haunted my soul as we
visited the National Memorial for Peace and Justice. It sits on a
grassy, six-acre hill on the outskirts of Montgomery, Alabama.
The "lynching memorial" bears witness to more than 4,400 African American men, women and children who were hanged,
burned alive, shot, drowned, or beaten to death by white mobs
between 1877 and 1950.

I stood in humbled silence beneath the eight-hundred sus-
pended blocks of Corten steel that bear the names of victims in
the counties where they were lynched. I found the ones that named
the Florida counties in which I have lived and served. Like Lady
Macbeth's failed attempt to wipe the blood from her hands, I recognized again that as a beneficiary of generations of white privilege, I still carry the inescapable stain of that past into the present.
I caught a new glimpse of what happened at Golgotha in light of
the horrifying reality of what happened at the lynching trees and
which, in its own way, still happens today.

It happened again during the long, hot summer of 2020 with
the murder of Ahmaud Arbery on a quiet road in Georgia, the
shooting of Breonna Taylor in her home in Louisville, and the

2. Cone, *Lynching Tree*, 73.

3. Cone, *Lynching Tree*, 63.

death of George Floyd on a street corner in Minneapolis. Even as Jesus cried, "I thirst!" we heard George Floyd cry, "I can't breathe!" Even as Jesus commended his mother into his disciple's care, we watched Floyd die with his mother's name on his lips.

I realized what Cone meant when he wrote, "The cross placed alongside the lynching tree can help us to see Jesus in America in a new light."[4] His insight gave me a deeper way of hearing the two times Jesus specifically recalled words from the Psalms while he was on the cross. One is the piercing cry of dereliction; the other is a daring exclamation of confident faith and hope.

Questions for Reflection

What is the most powerful image or picture of Jesus' crucifixion in your experience?

What do you know about the history of lynching in America?

How does the comparison between lynching and crucifixion speak to you?

"Jesus cried out with a loud voice, 'Eloi, Eloi, lema sabachthani?' which means, 'My God, my God, why have you forsaken me?'" (Mark 15:34 NRSV)

In the darkest hour of all the dark hours of human history, Jesus shouted to God the question that was the desperate cry of every tortured victim and the grief-filled cry of every family member who watched helplessly as their loved one suffered and died at the lynching tree. It is the question of every thoughtful person who confronts persistent injustice, innocent suffering, and unnecessary death in its multitude of diabolical forms in our world today.

How could the early Christians make sense of Jesus' God-forsaken cry? Why did the one who heard God say, "You are my beloved Son" suffer alone in the apparent absence of God? What

4. Cone, *Lynching Tree*, xix.

would they do with the crisis in Jesus' story that was too horrifying to remember but too important to forget?

Mark and Matthew included Jesus' cry in their passion narratives, but Luke and John left it out. Perhaps it was more than they or their readers could comprehend. Paul acknowledged that the very idea of the Son of God dying on a Roman lynching tree was "foolishness" (1 Cor 1:18–25). In the seventeenth century, John Milton found the passion story beyond his ability to express in poetry and "nothing satisfied with what was begun, left it unfinished"[5] A traditional passion hymn asks, "What language shall I borrow?"

How could African Americans make sense of suffering and injustice that was too deep for words beside the lynching tree? How can any of us make sense of the senseless, God-forsaken injustice and pain we see in others or experience for ourselves?

Roger Nelson was a seminary student when his parents traveled to Chicago to meet his fiancé. As was their custom, they went to worship on a glorious spring Sunday morning. On the way back to the parking lot, a crack addict shot and killed Nelson's father.

Well-intended seminary colleagues felt led to advise Nelson on how to find meaning in his father's death. We've all been like them, either struggling with our own tragedy or attempting to help other people deal with their suffering. It's a particularly persistent temptation for pastors who attempt to soften another person's loss or pain by offering simplistic spiritual platitudes or assuring them that God has a reason for everything.

The most helpful person for Nelson was a professor who had lost a son. The professor said that if God appeared in person and handed him a piece of paper with the reason for his son's death written on it, he would have crumpled it up, thrown it back in God's face, and said, "It isn't enough!" Thirty years later, Nelson said that none of the attempts to wring meaning out of his father's death were enough to justify or compensate for it.[6]

When I heard Nelson's story, I remembered the way Jesus shouted, "My God, why have you left me?" (Mark 15:34). Perhaps

5. Milton, "The Passion," *English Poetry*.
6. Nelson, "Episode 18."

as he experienced abject rejection and horrifying pain, Jesus was throwing it all back in God's face as if to say, "God, it's not worth this! It isn't enough!"

Perhaps in that moment Jesus felt that none of it—not God's affirmation at his baptism, not the vision of the Kingdom of God, not his faithful obedience to do God's will in God's way from his baptism in the Jordan to this horrendous moment on Golgotha—was enough to justify his suffering. None of it was enough to make sense of the way his life of love was nailed to the cross by the forces of hatred in a power-obsessed world. None of it was enough to touch the lonely anguish of the most God-forsaken hour in human history.

Hanging naked, beaten, and bleeding on a lynching tree, Jesus recalled words that were so deeply imbedded in his mind and heart that he instinctively shrieked them as he drifted in and out of consciousness.

> My God! My God,
>
> why have you left me all alone?
>
> Why are you so far from saving me—
>
> so far from my anguished groans?
>
> My God, I cry out during the day,
>
> but you don't answer. (Ps 22:1–2)

Psalm 22:1–21 records one of the most desperate prayers in all of Scripture. But the psalmist wasn't alone. The prophet Isaiah also prayed:

> Surely you are a god who hides himself,
>
> Israel's God and savior. (Isa 45:15)

We hear it again from Habakkuk:

> O LORD, how long shall I cry for help,
>
> and you will not listen?
>
> Or cry to you "Violence!"
>
> and you will not save? (Hab 1:1–2)

Theologians use the Latin phrase *Deus absconditus* to name the absence or hiddenness of God. After her death, we learned from Mother Teresa's journal that she went on for long periods of time feeling the absence of God. Episcopalian priest and biblical scholar Fleming Rutledge called it "a major theme of scripture and a common struggle in the Christian life." She warned, "Anyone who has not asked this question [My God, why?] hasn't been fully tested yet."[7]

If we are honest with ourselves and with God, we are within shouting distance of that moment at Golgotha when we come face to face with inexplicable suffering, raging injustice, life-draining loss, and the impenetrable darkness of death. Sooner or later, every follower of Christ who dares to pray for God's Kingdom to come and God's will to be done on earth will feel overwhelmed by the hypocrisy, racism, cruelty, and injustice of a sin-corrupted world. We are forced to confess the ways we are implicated in the suffering by our sins of omission or commission, by what we have done or left undone. The more deeply we believe in Jesus' teaching and the more closely we follow his way, the more intensely we feel the apparent absence and unutterable silence of God that reaches its nadir at the cross.

There is a time and place for academic study of the theories of the atonement, for in-depth biblical analysis or theological debate about what happened at Golgotha. But when we find our way to that place in our own souls, we discover that it is neither the time nor place for all of that. None of our words are strong enough to explain evil so bold, mystery so deep, suffering so great, and a love so strong. With Charles Wesley we sing in humbled awe, "O Love Divine, what hast thou done?"

But don't miss this: the words Jesus evoked from the Psalm are a prayer. Jesus joined the psalmists and prophets who hurled their cries of dereliction directly into the face of God. Their experience of the absence of God did not prevent them from praying to the God who was hidden in darkness. This was the faith of the

7. Rutledge, "Divine Absence."

anonymous victim of Nazi injustice who scratched the words onto a basement wall in Cologne, Germany:

> I believe in the sun even when it is not shining.
>
> I believe in love even when there is no one there.
>
> I believe in God even when he is silent.[8]

Then suddenly, the Psalm Jesus remembered surprises us by taking an unexpected turn from suffering toward hope in verses 21–31. The psalmist dares to believe that God is present in the mystery of God's absence.

> Because he didn't despise or detest
>
> the suffering of the one who suffered—
>
> he didn't hide his face from me.
>
> No, he listened when I cried out to him for help.
> (Ps 22:24)

Fleming Rutledge pointed out that in Jesus' cry of dereliction at the cross, we are left with the most profound paradox of the Christian faith.

> To know God in his Son Jesus Christ is to know that he is unconditionally love unto the last drop of God's own blood. In the cross and resurrection of his Son, God has given us everything that we need to live with alongside the terrors of his seeming absence.[9]

James Cone wrote that enslaved Blacks "seized on the power of the cross" because "Christ crucified manifested God's loving and liberating presence *in* the contradictions of black life."[10] Karl Barth, whose revolutionary theology was forged on the anvil of his opposition to Nazi ideology, similarly declared that "the *deity* of the *living* God . . . found its meaning and its power only . . . in His *togetherness* with [humanity]."[11] In a similar way, Roger

8. Quoted in Howe, "I Believe in the Sun."

9. Rutledge, "Divine Absence," para. 19.

10. Cone, *Lynching Tree*, 2.

11. Barth, *Humanity of God*, 45.

Nelson bore witness that knowing that God enters into our loss *is* enough. It was enough for him to know "God was as broken in this as I was." Nelson affirmed that he lives with the assurance that in the end "God will wipe away all the tears and that all of us, including my father and my father's murderer will somehow be wrapped up in God's peace."[12]

Questions for Reflection

Read Psalm 22. What emotions does it evoke for you?

How have you experienced the absence of God?

Where have you found God in your suffering?

Jesus' ruthlessly honest prayer to the God by whom he felt utterly forsaken sets our bearings on the word of hope Jesus exclaimed in the second psalm he remembered on the cross.

> "Crying out in a loud voice, Jesus said, 'Father, into your hands I entrust my life.' After he said this, he breathed for the last time." (Luke 23:46)

Jesus used the more impersonal word "God" in Psalm 22, but in recalling Psalm 31, he prayed to his "Father." The Aramaic *Abba* was the intimate, family word similar to "Papa" or "Daddy" in English. It was the name for God that Jesus used consistently throughout his ministry, the name with which he taught his followers to pray, the One to whom Jesus cried his desperate prayer in the Garden of Gethsemane (Matt 26:36–38). Now, with his final breath, he released himself into the arms of *Abba*, his heavenly Father, even as he had been cradled in the arms of his human *Abba*, Joseph.

I experienced the power of the *Abba* prayer in the death of my friend, John. We were nearly the same age at 38 and 39. We lived in the same suburban neighborhood, were charter members of the same Rotary Club, and sent our children to the same

12. Nelson, "Episode 18."

elementary school. John worked in professional staffing at Walt Disney World; I was a young pastor attempting to launch the new congregation in which his family participated. He was a day-brightening friend who made me feel that I was a better person than I thought I was whenever I was with him.

I wasn't prepared for the call. The melanoma we hoped had been defeated had returned with a vengeance. There was nothing to be done. I needed to get to the hospital right away. I prayed with his wife and mother before the doctors turned off the machines. Then I found my way in stunned silence to my car and slammed the door behind me. The click of the key in the ignition unlocked the flood of emotion I had held inside. I pounded my fist on the steering wheel and shouted with no one around to hear, "No! No! No!" In that experience of *Deus absconditus*, I was hurling my grief back into the face of the God whom I had learned from childhood to call "Father."

John's siblings asked that we end the memorial service by singing, "Now the Day Is Over." It was the hymn their parents sang as a lullaby when they tucked their children into bed. The last verse offers this word of hope.

> When the morning wakens,
> Then may I arise
> Pure, and fresh, and sinless
> In Thy holy eyes.[13]

That's when I learned that the words Jesus prayed from Psalm 31 may have been an evening or bedtime prayer. Perhaps Mary and Joseph repeated that prayer as Jesus fell asleep in their arms. Now, the Son of God recalled those words as he entrusted his life into the hands of the God he called *Abba*.

There is, however, a profound difference between my experience of *Deus absconditus* in the death of my friend and God's apparent absence at the lynching tree, whether it is on a hill called Golgotha or on a street corner in Minneapolis. The death of my

---

13. Young, *Book of Hymns*, 495.

friend falls into the category of what Hamlet called "the slings and arrows of outrageous fortune . . . The heart-ache and the thousand natural shocks / That flesh is heir to."[14] Cancer doesn't care who it attacks. Like the COVID-19 virus, they create equal-opportunity suffering, refusing to acknowledge any difference between my house and the White House.

By contrast, the injustice of the cross and the lynching tree are the direct result of the sin-twisted choices of real people. They are the end product of evil-infected institutions through the systems of politics, power, and economics that work their evil ways around us every day. They are a blatant denial of God's Kingdom vision, our outright rejection of Jesus' way of love and peace, and our self-destructive refusal to find our bearings in the way of Christ. Instead of leading us up to the Sermon on the Mount, they drag us out to Golgotha.

The Old Testament prophets opened the eyes of their people to the specific ways they participated in the rejection of God's purpose and the steps they needed to take to find their bearings into God's future. In our recent racial crisis, we were given contemporary prophets to name the sins of white supremacy and call us to a better future: William J. Barber II, Ibram X. Kendi, Robin DiAngelo, and Isabel Wilkerson.

As followers of Christ, we cannot stand on the sidelines and say we aren't there at the lynching tree. We cannot pretend that we didn't know the way the virus of white supremacy continues to work its destructive way in our souls, our relationships, and the sin-infected systems in our businesses, government, and churches. We are there at the lynching tree just as surely as we are there at the cross, bearing the weight of our sins both personally and within the systemic racism that still corrupts our culture. And at the cross, we can become the imperfect people through whom God's perfect love, forgiveness, and reconciliation can become a reality in our painfully broken world.

The words of Psalm 31 that Jesus gurgled into sound were neither the restful words of a childhood lullaby nor the weak

14. Shakespeare, *Hamlet*, act III, sc. I.

words of despairing resignation, but a bold declaration of absolute confidence and trust. The psalmist names the Lord as a "rock" and "fortress." The Psalm has the ring of an expectant demand of daring hope. The CEB uses no fewer than fourteen exclamation points to convey the energy with which the psalmist prays:

> I trust you, Lord!
>
> I affirm, "You are my God."
>
> My future is in your hands.
>
> Don't hand me over to my enemies,
>
> to all who are out to get me!
>
> Shine your face on your servant;
>
> save me by your faithful love! (Ps 31:14–16)

Luke captured the energy of the Hebrew text in saying that Jesus "cried out with a loud voice" (Luke 23:46). Psalm 31 is the exclamation of faithful men and women in every generation who have gone head to head with the devil, have wrestled with the worst our sin-broken world can do, have given it all they had, and who came to the end with the assurance that their efforts were not wasted. They believed that what they did made a difference. It was their part in the coming of the Kingdom of God.

These faithful Christ-followers may not have seen the perfect fulfillment of the God-inspired vision they followed, but they trusted God to complete God's work in the future. They held (or were held by) the faith that by God's resurrection power, there would be a new and better day ahead. They shared Paul's confidence that "the one who began a good work among you will bring it to completion by the day of Jesus Christ" (Phil 1:6 NRSV).

The Psalm concludes with powerful words that call us to face whatever life throws at us with our own small measure of the courageous confidence with which Jesus gulped his last earthly breath:

> All you who are faithful, love the Lord!
>
> The Lord protects those who are loyal,
>
> but he pays the proud back to the fullest degree.

All you who wait for the Lord,

be strong and let your heart take courage. (Ps 31:23–24)

Questions for Reflection

Read Psalm 31. How would you describe the emotions the psalmist expresses?

Why do you think Jesus invoked these words?

How does the Psalm speak to your life?

"Jesus called loudly, 'Father, I place my life
in your hands!'" (Luke 23:46 MSG)

Where did Jesus find the faith to utter the prayer from Psalm 31 at the end of his life? What if the way Jesus prayed at the end was a result of the way he lived? How might this Psalm be the way we find our bearings through the crises in our lives, as well?

I had never heard about the 1921 Tulsa massacre until the summer 2020 anniversary of the destruction of the Greenwood district, then known as "Black Wall Street." My ignorance of that crisis is another example of the sinister sins of white superiority that continue to hide the parts of our history we would like to ignore or avoid. Likewise, I had never heard of Ida B. Wells-Barnett who, during that same summer of 2020, was awarded a posthumous Pulitzer Prize for her investigative journalism on lynching.

Born six months before Lincoln issued the Emancipation Proclamation, her early life and education provide another witness to the way courageous people overcame the challenges of our nation's "original sin." She was a writer and editor for an African-American newspaper when the 1892 lynching of three friends—businessmen whose successful grocery store was an economic threat to white grocers in Memphis—inspired her to do research on lynching, often at risk to her own safety. She was relentlessly outspoken, even when the leaders of her African Methodist

Episcopal Church shunned her. When her life was in danger, she wrote in her journal, "I cannot help it . . . I trust God."[15]

Ida B. Wells-Barnett died of kidney disease in 1931 with her work largely pushed to the fringes of American history. But my sense is that whether or not she used the same words, she lived and died in the same trust with which both the psalmist and Jesus prayed, "Father, into your hands I entrust my life."

Here's my fresh insight into the final words Jesus recalled from the Old Testament. The psalmist's prayer was not only the way he died; it defined the way he lived. The trust to offer this prayer in the hour of his death was the cumulative confidence of having prayed these words and having lived by them throughout his life. His last breath was the final expression of the way he learned to trust God along the way.

Perhaps Mary and Joseph taught Jesus to pray, "Father, into your hands I trust my life" while they were refugees in Egypt, hiding from King Herod's wrath and not at all sure of what was ahead. Perhaps the prayer took root within him as he heard the Psalm repeated in the Nazareth synagogue. Perhaps he heard it discussed as a teenager in the Temple.

Perhaps when Jesus was baptized by John, the voice he heard over the water had become so familiar to him that his instinctive, internal response was, "Father, I trust my life to you." Perhaps during the long, lonely days in the wilderness every victory over temptation strengthened Jesus' confidence in the God to whom he had entrusted his life.

Perhaps by the time Jesus stepped out on the way that would lead inexorably to his suffering and death (Luke 9:51), he had prayed those words so often that they had become the internal compass that would keep him moving toward the True North of God's saving purpose regardless of the cost. Perhaps in the Garden of Gethsemane, in the blood and sweat of his desire to go some other way, he knew in ways he would never not know that he could rely on the God to whom he had learned to trust his life.

---

15. Cone, *Lynching Tree*, 130.

Perhaps the faith in which he died was the result of the faith in which he had lived.

After four decades of pastoral ministry, I'm convinced that people generally die the way they live. If a person has been bitter, self-absorbed, or just plain mean, they will come to the end of life with anger, frustration, and denial. But if they have lived with a continually maturing relationship with God, with love, joy, faith, and humble gratitude for the unexpected and undeserved gifts of God's grace, they will face death with persistent peace and obstinate hope.

I learned this lesson as a young, inexperienced, and overly self-confident pastor in my first appointment. After visiting a long-time member of the church who was painfully declining with terminal cancer, I told his son that I was sorry about what his father was facing. The son, a man of equally warm-hearted, genuine faith, corrected me by saying that his father was so grateful for all the good things he had been given in this life, that his father figured it was enough to be at peace as he came to the end.

I learned the lesson myself at forty-five years old when I was diagnosed with cardiomyopathy. The doctor told me that it is generally a terminal disease; its medical cure was a heart transplant. I survived without the transplant because of the wisdom and aggressive treatment by a superb cardiologist who credited my recovery to the people who prayed for me.

I had planned to be at Florida Field at the University of Florida cheering for the Gators rather than wondering about my survival in a cardiac care unit. I told my twin brother, "I feel like it's halftime in the locker room. I have every intention of being on the field for the rest of the game, but if not, it's been one hell of a good first half." Now, in the fourth quarter of my life, that crass expression of gratitude has only grown stronger along with my confidence in the God to whom I have continued to entrust my life.

Praying and living in the spirit of the Psalm, Jesus' last words are anything but passive resignation in the face of incomprehensible evil and injustice. This is neither a prayer of overly simplistic piety nor of a fatalistic belief that "God has a reason for everything." Praying this prayer is not an escape into an esoteric spirituality that avoids confrontation with the powers of personal sin, systemic evil, economic greed, nationalistic jingoism, or political partisanship. It is not a denial of our complicity in the same sins that nailed Jesus to a Roman cross, the same sins that left Black bodies dangling on lynching trees, the same sins that continue to plague our lives today.

Jesus' final shout from a parched throat and sun-blistered lips declares that the way we live and the way we die are held in the arms of a faithful God, who we have learned to trust with our lives. It is a prayer of uncalculating, unflinching, and almost unbelievable trust that reaches through the suffering and beyond the darkness to take hold of—or be held by—the absolute goodness, faithfulness, and steadfast love of the God who was with Jesus in his most God-forsaken hour. It is a shout of hope that "when the morning wakens," we will arise

Praying and living this prayer means daring to believe that God is with us in the ultimate paradox of the cross; that in ways we may not see, God is able to wrench good out of evil, hope out of despair, and life out of death. Living in the spirit of the psalmist's prayer challenges us to believe in what Martin Luther King Jr. announced as God's ability to use unmerited suffering as a "creative force . . . the power of God unto social and individual salvation."[16]

Dr. King's confidence in the "creative force" of God's love at the cross inspires us to engage in essential practices of spiritual discipline, personal growth, and social justice, which, when practiced over time, will enable us to "go from strength to strength" (Ps 84:7) in a growing assurance that the way Jesus walked and the way he calls us to follow is the way that leads to the completion (*teleios*) of God's transformation of the kingdoms of this world into the Kingdom of God.

Following the way that Jesus walked leads inexorably to our own Golgotha where we learn to pray as John Wesley taught us:

---

16. King, *Testament of Hope*, 41–42.

I am no longer my own, but thine.

Put me to what thou wilt, rank me with whom thou wilt.

Put me to doing, put me to suffering.

Let me be employed by thee or laid aside for thee,

exalted for thee or brought low for thee.

Let me be full, let me be empty.

Let me have all things, let me have nothing.

I freely and heartily yield all things

to thy pleasure and disposal.

And now, O glorious and blessed God,

Father, Son, and Holy Spirit,

thou art mine, and I am thine. So be it.

And the covenant which I have made on earth,

let it be ratified in heaven. Amen.[17]

17. Young, *United Methodist Hymnal*, 607.

6

Walking the Emmaus Way

Read: Luke 24:1–35

T imothy Egan hoped to find his bearings on the way of faith when he walked the *Via Francigena*, the 1,056-mile-long path from Canterbury to Rome that pilgrims have followed since Sigerico, the Archbishop of Canterbury, shared the journal of his pilgrimage in 990 CE. Egan recounted his pilgrimage in his book *A Pilgrimage to Eternity*. By the end of his journey, *The New York Times* columnist had learned, "It helps to walk with eyes open—otherwise you miss the breadcrumbs of epiphany along the way." He concluded with words that are sometimes attributed to St. Julian, the patron saint of wanderers and hospitallers, "The way is made by walking."[1]

We've been making our way by walking the way Jesus walked. We've walked through crucial moments when he found his bearings in the Hebrew Scriptures. We've walked the way that led inevitably to Golgotha where his story seemed to end, but a new story was about to begin for two disciples who were making their way by walking the road to Emmaus.

1. Egan, *Pilgrimage to Eternity*, 327–28.

"It is finished." (John 19:30 NRSV)

When Jesus said, "It is finished," his followers believed it! His male disciples could not face the ghastly sight of the teacher they hoped might be the Messiah beaten to a pulp and hanging on a Roman cross. They ran away before Jesus used his last breath to utter the words of Psalm 31. Only the women hung in there to the end, perhaps hoping against hope that the story would not end the way it did.

Perhaps Jesus' followers hoped he would prove his God-given identity when the crowd shouted, "Let him save himself if he really is the Christ sent from God" (Luke 23:35). Perhaps, in spite of Jesus' multiple predictions, they still hoped he would respond to the cry of the criminal hanging next to him, "Aren't you the Christ? Save yourself and us!" (Luke 23:39).

But Jesus did not save himself nor, it appeared in the crisis, anyone else. He did not come down from the cross in miraculous, God-like power, the way Satan tempted him in the wilderness. He came down like every helpless victim of mob-incited violence —when they pried the nails from his hands and feet and dropped his blood-soaked body into the arms of Joseph of Arimathea (Luke 23:50–53).

By all the available evidence, Jesus was finished—lynched by the forces of political power, systematic evil and religious jealousy. His vision of the Kingdom of God was shattered by the competing kingdoms of this earth. His words of love were silenced by shouts of hatred; his acts of compassion negated by human cruelty. His way of truth was strung up as a lie.

Talk about losing their bearings! For his disciples, walking the way Jesus walked was finished. Everything they had seen, hoped, or dared to believe was gone. All they could do was stare blindly at each other in soul-numbing grief too deep for words. Emily Dickinson caught the feeling of the moment when she wrote, "After great pain, a formal feeling comes— / The Nerves sit ceremonious, like Tombs."[2]

2. Dickinson, "After Great Pain."

Jesus' followers were neither the first people nor the last to face the great pain of the unjust death of their leader. John Lewis never forgot the moment he heard that Martin Luther King Jr. had been shot. "I was obliterated, blown beyond any sensations whatsoever. I was numb. Frozen. Stunned stock-still, inside and out . . . Dr. King was my friend, my brother, my leader . . . the one who opened my eyes to the world . . . He made me who I *am*."[3]

Two months later, Lewis was in the Ambassador Hotel in Los Angeles with Robert F. Kennedy's campaign team when the man he hoped would become president died on the hotel kitchen floor. "I was crying, sobbing, heaving as if something had been busted open inside. I sat on the floor dazed, rocking back and forth . . . saying one word out loud, over and over again, 'Why? Why? Why?'"[4]

Jesus' disciples experienced the pain, disappointment, and grief that recur with disturbing regularity in our hate-soaked, racism-ridden, violence-addicted world. Then, the unbelievable happened! The morning after the Sabbath, their grief was disrupted by the preposterous report of what the women said they had seen and heard at the tomb. Even Peter's quick inspection of the tomb solved nothing and left him "wondering what had happened" (Luke 24:12).

Everything they assumed was nailed down—both literally and figuratively—was coming loose. Jesus' story was not finished! It was unhinged like the dangling, fear-driven nonending of Mark's Gospel (Mark 16:8). They knew how to deal with death, but they did not have a clue what to do with rumors of resurrection. The recently vacated tomb did not, in and of itself, provide assurance that Christ was risen. In every case, it took more than an open grave for Jesus' followers to believe that he was alive and walking the way with them.

---

3. Meacham, *Truth Is Marching*, 228.
4. Meacham, *Truth Is Marching*, 230–1.

Questions for Reflection

How have you made your way by walking?

*What is your sense of how the disciples responded to Jesus'
death?*

*When have you experienced the pain or loss John Lewis
described?*

"On that same day, two disciples were traveling
to a village called Emmaus." (Luke 24:13)

As the sun was setting on a day Cleopas and his unnamed companion never anticipated and would never forget, they headed for
home. The text is unclear, but some have suggested that Cleopas's
companion may have been his wife, perhaps a woman named
Mary who was at the cross (John 19:25). They were walking to
Emmaus, a few miles west of Jerusalem.

The fact that they were walking toward the setting sun might
help explain why their tear-drained eyes didn't recognize the
stranger who walked with them. Their eyes were not opened to
see "the breadcrumbs of epiphany along the way." Jesus entered
their story unobtrusively. There were no angels, no earthquake,
no trumpets, no massed choirs singing Handel's "Hallelujah," no
sanctuary-full congregation shouting, "He is risen, indeed!" Jesus
quietly "joined them on their journey." They had no idea that the
one walking with them was their Risen Lord.

This is a good place to pause the action and ask how many
times the Risen Christ has walked with us through the dark nights
of our souls but our eyes were not opened to realize his presence.

Paul Young imagined a conversation in *The Shack* when
Mack asked Jesus, "Does that mean that all roads will lead to
you?" Jesus smiled and replied, "Not at all . . . Most roads don't
lead anywhere. What it does mean is that I will travel any road
to find you."[5] Parker Palmer came to the same awareness through

5. Young, *Shack*, 182.

his bouts with depression. He affirmed, "The God I'm familiar with . . . accompanies me as I try to grope my way through the darkest of dark places."[6]

Is it possible that even when we cannot see, hear, or feel his presence, the living Christ is walking along with us? How often do we fail to catch sight of the "breadcrumbs of epiphany" along our way?

Back on the Emmaus Road, Jesus opened the conversation with a peculiar question, "What are you discussing with each other while you walk along?" It was like asking people in Manhattan what they were talking about as they walked up 5th Avenue on the weekend after 9/11. What else could they talk about? Rehearsing the same story over and over again is a normal part of the grief process. It's our attempt to shape sense out of nonsense, to make that which is unmanageable manageable. Was this stranger the only person in Jerusalem who had not heard the story?

Jesus listened. The Risen Lord entered into the story of their loss, grief, sorrow, and confusion. He heard them speak some of the most painful words anywhere in Scripture.

"We had hoped he was the one to redeem Israel."
(Luke 24:21)

John Greenleaf Whittier, the Quaker poet and abolitionist, wrote:

Of all sad words of tongue or pen,

The saddest are these: "It might have been!"[7]

Luke used the Greek verb indicating action that was completed in the past; finished, over and done, never to happen again. "We had hoped" indicates that at one time, they actually had hoped.

They had hoped Jesus was the promised One through whom Israel would be redeemed.

They had hoped Jesus would break the heavy-handed rule of Roman authority and set God's people free.

6. Palmer, *Brink of Everything*, 97.

7. Whittier, "Maud Muller."

They had hoped the prayer he taught them would be answered; that God's kingdom would come; and God's will would be done here, on earth, right now, among them.

They had hoped that by divine power Jesus would be protected from the suffering and death he predicted.

Now, the only thing they could say was, "We had hoped."

Jesus' reply may at first sound like a cruel rebuke, "You foolish people! Your dull minds keep you from believing all that the prophets talked about" (Luke 24:25). But because of the way Jesus is portrayed in the rest of the story, I hear it as an expression of infinite patience with the limitations of our human understanding. The Risen Christ understands how hard it can be for us to believe.

Let's face it, if we find the gospel easy to believe, we haven't actually heard how peculiar, radical, and disruptive it is. If we can meld Jesus' words comfortably into our lives without being unsettled by the way he challenges some of our most commonly held assumptions, we haven't been listening. If we can stand at the cross without shouting, "My God, why?" and if we can believe that Christ is risen without having troubling doubts or honest questions, we may not be ready to follow a Risen Lord.

This may be why Thomas's story made the cut to be included in the post-resurrection narratives (John 20:24–29). It's the kind of story media-savvy editors in our image-conscious culture might have tucked away in an investigative report that few people would ever read.

Thomas holds a place for everyone who wrestles with doubt and searches for a faith that makes sense in our brains and a difference in our lives. Thomas demonstrates that honest doubt is not the opposite of faith but can become an essential step along the way of a growing, maturing faith in the Risen Christ.

If Jesus is alive, released from the tomb, and out there on the road ahead of us (Mark 16:7), the opposite of faith is not doubt, but an overly simplistic, unthinking certainty that nails things down as firmly as Jesus was nailed to a cross and freezes things in place with the rigid coldness of a stone-sealed tomb. It's the narrow self-assurance that locks the upper room door to the surprising presence of a Risen Christ who shows up when we least expect him and is always calling his disciples to get up and follow him on the way to places we never imagined, expected, or particularly wanted to go.

In his archetypical novel, *East of Eden*, John Steinbeck portrayed this kind of religious rigidity in Liza Hamilton. Steinbeck described her as "a tight hard little women as humorless as a chicken . . . [with] a code of morals that pinned down and beat the brains out of nearly everything that was pleasant to do."[8]

I was assaulted by folks like Liza one Monday after Easter. They heard a rumor that in an adult Sunday School class the day before, an active, long-time church member confessed, "I can't believe in the resurrection." They wanted me to set him straight along with the rest of the class on the necessity of belief in the resurrection.

These well-meaning but overly self-confident believers were not satisfied when I pointed out that the disciples had a hard time believing it. Some were still doubting at the ascension (Matt 28:17). I assured them that if there was a place in the upper room for Thomas, there was a place in our church for folks who have a hard time believing it as well.

They were even more aggravated when I recommended that the class study Leslie Weatherhead's classic, *The Christian Agnostic*. The title alone gave them apoplexy! Weatherhead recommended that we file the things we have a hard time believing in a mental box labeled, "Awaiting Further Light." In the meantime, he encouraged us to follow Jesus on the basis of what we can believe and join other followers in walking the way Jesus walked in the way Jesus walked it.[9]

By the next Easter, those Liza Hamilton-like believers had found their way to a church that didn't have room for a "Doubting Thomas." But even as Jesus honored Thomas's doubts and invited him to check out the evidence for himself, he welcomed

---

8. Steinbeck, *East of Eden*, 10.

9. Weatherhead, *Christian Agnostic*, 21.

Cleopas and his companion to find their way while walking with him on the way to Emmaus.

> "He interpreted for them the things written about him
> in all the scriptures." (Luke 24:27)

I was surprised to discover that Jesus' dying prayer from Psalm 31 is the last time he specifically quotes the Old Testament in the Gospels. Luke includes two indirect references to the Hebrew Scriptures in the post-resurrection stories. He writes that on the way to Emmaus, "[Jesus] interpreted for them the things written about himself in all the scripture, starting with Moses and going through all the Prophets" (Luke 24:27). It must have been quite a journey! Luke also says that later, in the upper room, "He opened their minds to understand the scriptures" (Luke 24:45). But we do not hear words from Scripture on Jesus' lips again.

New Testament scholar Richard Hays opened my mind to understand this abrupt change in the text when he explained, "We come to know Jesus in Luke only as his *narrative identity* is enacted in and through the story." He said the Gospels invite us to "become participants in the story that we read and narrate anew."[10]

My application of Hays's advice is that we do not experience the Risen Christ solely through biblical prooftexts, propositional truths, or doctrinal affirmations (as important as those are). We experience the transformative presence of the Risen Christ through narrative engagement in his story. We get to know Jesus by walking with him along the way he walked, just as the Israelites came to know God as they walked the circuitous way from Egypt to the Promised Land. Even as Jesus found his bearings in recalling stories for the Hebrew tradition, followers of Christ find their bearings in recalling, rehearsing, and living into Jesus' story.

I came to the conviction that Jesus no longer evoked words from Scripture because in the resurrection he became the living Word, present and at work among us. Jesus said he did not come "to do away with the Law and the Prophets . . . but to *fulfill* them"

10. Hays, *Reading Backwards*, 57, 16.

(Matt 5:17; emphasis mine). The writer of Hebrews opened the letter with this bold affirmation:

> In the past, God spoke through the prophets to our ancestors in many times and many ways. In these final days, though, he spoke to us through a Son. God made his Son the heir of everything . . . the imprint of God's being. He maintains everything with his powerful message. (Heb 1:1–3)

The essential core of God's will and way revealed in the long story of God's relationship with the covenant people were telescoped into the words, will, and way of Jesus in the context of his life, death, and resurrection. Paul declared, "The divine 'yes' has at last sounded him, for in him is the 'yes' that affirms all the promises of God" (2 Cor 1:19–20 MOFF). Jürgen Moltmann applied this insight to our experience when he wrote:

> The way of Christ comes into being under the feet of the person who walks it. To tread the way of Christ means believing in him. Believing in him means going with him along the part of the road he is taking at the present moment.[11]

I've long asserted that biblical faith has more to do with our feet than our heads. We don't "lose our heads" in simplistic spirituality or esoteric mysticism. We "use our heads" by learning to hear the Scriptures as they are interpreted through Christian tradition and shared in community with other disciples. Faith is not determined solely by the knowledge we hold in our brains but by the direction our feet are walking.

The writer of the Epistle to the Hebrews defined faith by describing the way Abraham "obeyed when he was called to go . . . and went out without knowing where he was going" (Heb 11:8). Faith is the way we respond to the challenge, "Strengthen your drooping hands and weak knees! Make straight paths for your feet" (Heb 12:12). Faith is the way we "run the race that is

---

11. Moltmann, *Way of Jesus*, 34.

laid out before us . . . [fixing] our eyes on Jesus, faith's pioneer and perfecter" (Heb 12:1–2).

Faith is the way we "carry out our own salvation" in the assurance that "God is the One who enables [us] both to want and to actually live out his good purposes" (Phil 2:12–13). Living by faith means making our way by walking with Jesus, along the way Jesus walked in the way Jesus walked it. The written Scriptures are inspired commentary, "useful one way or another—showing us truth, exposing our rebellion, correcting our mistakes, training us to live God's way" (2 Tim 3:16 MSG).

Questions for Reflection

How does the story of "Doubting Thomas" speak to you?

When have you experienced the kind of rigidity Steinbeck described in Liza Hamilton?

What difference does it make for you to get to know Jesus by walking with him?

"He took the bread, blessed and broke it, and gave it to them. Their eyes were opened and they recognized him."
(Luke 24:30–32)

Luke, the master storyteller, builds the narrative toward its dramatic climax at the dinner table when Jesus "took the bread, blessed and broke it, and gave it to them." The eucharistic phrases from early Christian worship must have awakened Luke's first readers like a surprising burst of fresh air blowing in from the Sea of Galilee on a spring morning. David Brooks would describe it as one of those "moments of porousness . . . when some mystical intrusion pierced through . . . and the world of eternity stepped into time."[12] Ordinary bread became a sacrament, the tangible expression of the intangible presence of the Risen Christ, the outward and visible sign of an inward and spiritual grace.

12. Brooks, *Second Mountain*, 231, 234.

Don't miss Luke's use of the passive voice. The disciples's grief-blinded *eyes were opened*, not by their own power, but by the God who, Isaiah promised, would "open blind eyes" (Isa 42:7). Easter faith begins with the evidence of the empty tomb, but experiencing the presence of the Risen Christ is a Spirit-empowered gift consistent with Jesus' words to Peter: "Flesh and blood has not revealed this to you, but my Father in heaven" (Matt 16:17 NRSV).

The opening of the Emmaus disciples' eyes drew me back to Paul's explosive prayer

> that the eyes of your heart will have enough light to see what is the hope of God's call . . . and what is the overwhelming greatness of God's power that is working among us believers . . . God's power was at work in Christ when God raised him from the dead. (Eph 1:18–20)

Our traditional communion liturgies take us to the Passover table where we "proclaim the Lord's death until he comes" (1 Cor 11:23–26). That's true. But what happened at the Emmaus table breaks into the darkness of Jesus' death with the transformative light of his resurrection. The sacrament is not only a place for repentance but also a feast of joyful celebration in which the one whose body was broken becomes the host at the celebration of his victory over suffering, sin, and death. Around his table we proclaim the mystery of faith: Christ has died. Christ is risen. Christ will come again.

It is not too much to hope that when we gather at the Lord's table, the same Spirit-infused energy that opened the eyes of the disciples in the breaking of bread at the Emmaus table will open our eyes to experience Christ alive in the ordinary places of our lives; taking whatever we have to offer, blessing us, breaking us, and giving us as a gift of God's love to the world. The taste of the bread on our tongues becomes a foretaste of a heavenly feast that is yet to come.

After their eyes were opened, Cleopas and his companion realized that Jesus had been with them all along the way. They saw the way the Risen Christ entered into their story of disappointment, death, and doubt. They remembered the way he put his story in the larger frame of the older story of God's journey with the Hebrew people. And in the breaking of the bread, he enabled them to see their own story in a whole new way. The stale bread of their past became the living bread of hope for their future.

In that eye-opening moment, they looked at each other in surprise as they asked, "Weren't our hearts on fire when he spoke to us along the road and when he explained the scriptures for us?" (Luke 24:32).

John Wesley had a similar experience in a small Bible study group meeting on Aldersgate Street in London. Wesley recorded that while they were discussing Paul's letter to Rome, "I felt my heart strangely warmed. I felt I did trust in Christ, Christ alone, for salvation; and an assurance was given me that He had taken away my sins, even mine, and saved me from the law of sin and death."[13]

Wesley's "heartwarming" experience was not the beginning of his story. It began as a child in the rectory at Epworth just as Jesus' story began as a child in Nazareth. God had been present and at work in Wesley's life all along the way, even when he was not fully aware of it.

Nor was Aldersgate the end or completion of Wesley's story. There would be many more eye-opening and heartwarming experiences for him in the years ahead. There is always a past and a future for every person who walks in the way of Jesus. But what happened at Aldersgate, like what happened around the table in Emmaus, was a crucial moment along the way when Wesley, with Cleopas and his companion, found their bearings as they followed the Risen Christ into an unexpected and unpredictable future.

Questions for Reflection

When have you experienced an eye-opening moment in your spiritual journey?

What difference does it make for you to experience the Lord's Supper from the perspective of the Emmaus story?

13. Wesley, *Journal*, 36.

How can you identify with Wesley's "heartwarming" experience?

"They got up right then and returned to Jerusalem."
(Luke 24:33)

Does it surprise you that Cleopas and his companion got up right then, left the dirty dishes on the dinner table, and headed back to Jerusalem?

The sun had set; darkness enveloped them. They had no idea what awaited them in the city where they, along with the other disciples, had been hiding in fear, like escaped slaves hiding in a darkened attic along the Underground Railroad. Would the same Roman power that crucified Jesus be on the lookout for his followers? Would the same angry mob that lynched Jesus come for them?

They had every reason to assume that the other disciples were still wrapped in somber sadness; still overwhelmed with grief; still swallowed up in the dark shadows of defeat, disappointment, and death; still in confusion about the empty tomb; still wondering what on earth had happened to Jesus' body; and not at all sure what they should do now.

As I walked through the story, I became more aware of the significance of that crucial moment when they got up, left their table, and headed to Jerusalem. Even with their freshly opened eyes and strangely warmed hearts, why would they rush back into the city that night? Wouldn't it have made more sense to get a good night's sleep and hit the road in the morning? What motivated them to leave a familiar past behind and step into an unknown future?

I was brooding over that question during my walk on a spectacular spring morning when I remembered an evocative phrase: *The Expulsive Power of a New Affection.* It was the title and theme of a book by Thomas Chalmers, the nineteenth-century pastor, economist, politician, and unrelenting advocate for the poor in Scotland. My interpretation of Chalmers's message is that changes of orientation do not happen solely on the basis of the negation or denial of evil, although it is necessary to clearly identify the life-destroying powers that are very much alive around, among, and within us.

That's why the baptismal liturgy begins by asking us to "renounce the spiritual forces of wickedness, reject the evil powers of this world, and repent of [our] sin." The present-tense verbs point to our continuing need to reset our internal compass on True North when we lose our bearings along the way. Everyone who chooses to follow Jesus has something they need to repentantly renounce and forcefully reject at crisis points in their journey. For example, any reckoning with the persistent evil of systemic racism demands that we who inherited the benefits of white privilege must clearly confess and painfully confront the continuing effects of its deadly virus in our lives, relationships, economy, politics, and culture.

But the 1980s "Just Say No" campaign demonstrated that just saying "no" is never enough. We cannot defeat the power of sin or follow the Risen Christ on the way that leads to life by repentance and rejection alone. The rejection of evil can take us to the tomb, but it does not release the power of resurrection. No one in the Gospels met Christ inside the tomb. They experienced the Risen Lord when they left the tomb behind. So, the baptismal liturgy goes on to call us to "accept the freedom and power God gives [us] to resist evil, injustice and oppression in whatever forms they present themselves." We courageously "confess Jesus Christ as [our] Savior, put [our] whole trust in his grace, and promise to serve him as [our] Lord, in union with the church which Christ has opened to people of all ages, nations, and races."[14]

Fans of Garrison Keillor's tales of Lake Woebegone may remember Larry the Sad Boy who "threw himself weeping and contrite on God's throne of grace on twelve separate occasions" in the Lutheran Church. Keillor said, "Even we fundamentalists got tired of him . . . God didn't mean for us to feel guilt all our

14. Young, *United Methodist Hymnal*, 34.

lives. There comes a point when you should dry your tears . . . and be of some good."[15]

There come moments for us like this moment for Cleopas and his companion when the "expulsive power" that is nothing less than the power that raised Jesus from the grave sets us out on the road again. We are drawn forward by the force of a "new affection," a greater love, a higher purpose, a nobler dream. We are not driven from the darkness so much as we are drawn toward the light. In the power of the resurrection, we receive freedom and power to serve the world, not by ourselves, but in union with every other follower of the Risen Lord.

Paul affirmed the total reorientation of his life when he un-abashedly renounced all of his human accomplishments and celebrated "the expulsive power" of his new affection for Jesus Christ:

> These things were my assets, but I wrote them off as a loss for the sake of Christ. But even beyond that, I consider everything a loss in comparison with the superior value of knowing Christ Jesus my Lord. I have lost everything for him, but what I lost I think of as sewer trash, so that I might gain Christ . . .
>
> It's not that I have already reached this goal or have already been perfected, but I pursue it, so that I may grab hold of it because Christ grabbed hold of me . . . I do this one thing: I forget about the things behind me and reach out for the things ahead of me. The goal I pursue is the prize of God's upward call in Christ Jesus. (Phil 3:7–14)

When Frederick Buechner delivered the commencement address at Union Theological Seminary, he reminded the graduates that "one way or another the road starts off from passion—a passion for what is holy and hidden, a passion for Christ . . . Scales fall from the eyes. A world within the world flames up." He went on to say that passion alone isn't enough. Even as Jesus helped Cleopas and his companion find their bearings in Hebrew Scriptures, Buechner advised the graduates preparing to go into ministry,

---

15. Keillor, *Leaving Home*, 182–83.

"Passion must be grounded, or like lightning without a lightning rod it can blow fuses and burn the house down." He asserted:

> The power that first stirs the heart must become the power that also stirs the hands and feet because it is the places your feet take you to and the work you find for your hands that finally proclaims who you are and who Christ is. Passion without wisdom to give it shape and direction is as empty as wisdom without passion to give it power and purpose.[16]

Questions for Reflection

What do you think motivated Cleopas and his companion to go back to Jerusalem?

How have you experienced "the expulsive power of a new affection"?

Where is the Risen Christ leading you now?

"It is completed." (John 19:30)

I'm not the only preacher who, on Easter morning, declared that the worst thing that happens is never the last thing. The New Testament declares that the last thing is and always will be resurrection. In the power of resurrection, we can hear Jesus' last words in the traditional translations—"It is finished"—as his best words when translated, "It is completed!"

The Greek word *telelestai* means to bring to an end, to complete, or to accomplish. It appeared in legal documents to indicate that the work was done, the agreement had been fulfilled. It's the word a runner shouts with arms raised at the finish line of a marathon. It's the way I felt when we arrived at the summit of Lion's Head and looked out over Cape Town. It comes from the same root word as *teleios*, the word with which Jesus named the end

16. Buechner, *Room Called Remember*, 146–47.

or goal of our discipleship in the Sermon on the Mount when he said, "Just as your heavenly Father is complete in showing love to everyone, so also you must be complete" (Matt 5:48).

But get this. In John's Gospel, the verb is in the perfect tense, describing an action that was completed in the past but has a continuing impact in the present. Christian hope is the confident expectation that God is at work in the present to complete in the future the soul-saving, life-redeeming, creation-healing work God began in the past. It affirms that the mission Jesus completed at the cross continues to be the mission to which the Risen Christ is calling us.

Resurrection is not only something God finished at Joseph's empty tomb; resurrection is the precursor of God's "great gettin' up morning" when the whole creation will be completed and made new; when the kingdoms of this earth really do become the Kingdom of our Lord and he reigns forever and ever (Rev 11:15). Easter is the first day of God's yet-to-be-completed creation.

The worst word is never the last word. The last word is always resurrection! We find our bearings as we walk the way Jesus walked in the way Jesus walked it, knowing that it is the way that leads to new life.

Resurrection never ends, but books do. I know of no better way to end this one than with the words of Charles Wesley's explosive Easter hymn.

> Soar we now where Christ has led, Alleluia!
>
> Following our exalted Head, Alleluia!
>
> Made like him, like him we rise, Alleluia!
>
> Ours the cross, the grave, the skies, Alleluia![17]

And so may it be as we walk the way that leads to resurrection!

---

17. Young, *United Methodist Hymnal*, 302.

Bibliography

"Arthur Brooks at National Prayer Breakfast." *C-Span*, February 6, 2020. https://www.c-span.org/video/?c4853002/user-clip-arthur-brooks-national-prayer-breakfast.

Barth, Karl. *The Humanity of God.* Louisville: Westminster John Knox, 1960.

Bonhoeffer, Dietrich. *The Collected Sermons of Dietrich Bonhoeffer.* Edited by Isabel Best. Minneapolis: Fortress, 2012.

Brooks, David. *The Second Mountain: The Quest for a Moral Life.* New York: Random House, 2019.

Browning, Robert. "Andrea del Sarto." *Poetry Foundation.* https://www.poetryfoundation.org/poems/43745/andrea-del-sarto.

Buechner, Fredrick. *A Room Called Remember.* New York: Harper & Row, 1984.

Chalmers, Thomas. *The Expulsive Power of a New Affection.* Wheaton: Crossway, 2020.

Chilcote, Paul, and Steve Harper. *Living Hope: An Inclusive Vision for the Future.* Eugene, OR: Cascade, 2020.

Coffin, William Sloane. *Living the Truth in a World of Illusions.* New York: Harper & Row, 1985.

Cone, James H. *The Cross and the Lynching Tree.* Maryknoll, NY: Orbis, 2011.

Dickinson, Emily. "After Great Pain A Formal Feeling Comes–372." *Poetry Foundation.* https://www.poetryfoundation.org/poems/47651/after-great-pain-a-formal-feeling-comes-372.

Egan, Timothy. *A Pilgrimage to Eternity.* New York: Viking, 2019.

Elizabeth, Queen. "Annus Horribilis Speech." *The Royal Houeshold*, November 24, 1992. https://www.royal.uk/annus-horribilis-speech.

Francis. *Christmas Greetings to the Roman Curia.* Vatican website. December 21, 2019. http://www.vatican.va/content/francesco/en/speeches/2019/december/documents/papa-francesco_20191221_curia-romana.html.

Franklyn, Paul, ed. *The United Methodist Book of Worship.* Nashville: Abingdon, 1992.

Freedman, David Noel. *The Anchor Bible Dictionary.* Vol. 3, *H–J.* New York: Doubleday, 1992.

George, Bill. *True North: Discover Your Authentic Leadership.* San Francisco: Jossey-Bass, 2007.

Gomes, Peter. *The Scandalous Gospel of Jesus.* New York: HarperCollins, 2007.

Harnish, James A. *A Disciple's Heart.* Nashville: Abingdon, 2015.

———. *A Disciple's Path.* Nashville: Abingdon, 2012.

Hays, Richard. *Reading Backwards.* Waco: Baylor University Press, 2014.

Howe, Everett. "I Believe in the Sun, Part I: Look Away." *The Humanist Seminarian,* March 19, 2017. https://humanistseminarian.com/2017/03/19/i-believe-in-the-sun-part-i-look-away/.

Jacobs, A. J. *The Year of Living Biblically.* New York: Simon & Schuster, 2008.

Johnston, Mark. *Saving God: Religion after Idolatry.* New Jersey: Princeton University Press, 2009.

Jones, E. Stanley. *The Christ of the Mount.* Nashville: Abingdon, 1981.

Keillor, Garrison. *Leaving Home: A Collection of Lake Wobegon Stories.* New York: Viking, 1987.

Kendi, Ibram X. *How to Be an Anti-Racist.* New York: One World, 2019.

Kennedy, Robert F. "Remarks on the Assassination of Martin Luther King, Jr." *American Rhetoric,* February 15, 2021. https://www.americanrhetoric.com/speeches/rfkonmlkdeath.html.

King, Martin Luther, Jr. *The Autobiography of Martin Luther King, Jr.* Edited by Clayborne Carson. New York: Warner, 2001.

———. *A Testament of Hope: The Essential Writings of Martin Luther King, Jr.* Edited by James Melvin Washington. New York: Harper & Row, 1986.

Kulick, Erik. "Using the Outdoors to Find Your Bearings." *True North: Wilderness Survival School,* May 7, 2015. https://www.exploretruenorth.com/using-the-outdoors-to-find-your-bearings/.

Küng, Hans, *On Being a Christian.* Garden City: Doubleday, 1976.

Lewis, C. S. *Mere Christianity.* New York: Macmillan, 1952.

———. *The Screwtape Letters.* New York: Macmillan, 1961.

Lincoln, Abraham. "Second Inaugural Address." *Our Documents.* https://www.ourdocuments.gov/doc.php?flash=false&doc=38&page=transcript.

Meacham, Jon. *His Truth is Marching On: John Lewis and the Power of Hope.* New York: Random House, 2020.

———. "Historian Jon Meacham remembers Rep. John Lewis." *Today,* July 18, 2020. https://www.today.com/video/historian-jon-meacham-remembers-rep-john-lewis-he-was-a-genuine-saint-87924293858.

Merton, Thomas. *Essential Writings.* Edited by Christine M. Bochen. Maryknoll: Orbis, 2002.

———. *The Inner Experience.* New York: HarperCollins, 2003.

Milton, John. *The Passion.* English Poetry. http://spenserians.cath.vt.edu/TextRecord.php?action=GET&textsid=37082.

Moffatt, James. *The New Testament.* New York: Association, 1922.

Moltmann, Jürgen. *The Way of Jesus Christ.* Minneapolis: Fortress, 1993.

Neal, Jerusha. *The Overshadowed Preacher: Mary, the Holy Spirit, and the Labor of Proclamation.* Grand Rapids: Eerdmans, 2020.

Nelson, Roger. "Episode 18: Roger Nelson." *Christian Century*, March 6, 2016. https://www.christiancentury.org/blogs/archive/2016-03/episode-18-roger-nelson.

Palmer, Parker. *On the Brink of Everything.* Oakland, CA: Berrett-Koehler, 2018.

Peterson, Eugene. *The Jesus Way: A Conversation on the Ways that Jesus is the Way.* Grand Rapids: Eerdmans, 2007.

———. *The Message: The New Testament in Contemporary Language.* Colorado Springs: NavPress, 1993.

Rendle, Gil. *Quietly Courageous: Leading the Church in a Changing World,* Lanham, MD: Rowman & Littlefield, 2019.

Robinson, Daniel, and Dan Johnson. *Misty Mornings and Grace-Filled Evenings.* Murrells Inlet, SC: Covenant, 2019.

Rutledge, Fleming. "Divine absence and the light inaccessible." *Christian Century*, August 27, 2018. https://www.christiancentury.org/article/critical-essay/divine-absence-and-light-inaccessible.

Shakespeare, William. *Four Tragedies: Hamlet, Othello, King Lear, and Macbeth.* New York: Penguin Classics, 1995.

Stavridis, James. *Sailing True North: Ten Admirals and the Voyage of Character.* New York: Penguin, 2019.

Steinbeck, John. *East of Eden.* New York: Penguin, 1979.

Underwood, Ron, dir. *City Slickers.* Los Angeles: Columbia Pictures, 1991.

The United Methodist Hymnal. Nashville, TN: United Methodist Publishing House, 1989.

Weatherhead, Leslie. *The Christian Agnostic.* Nashville: Abingdon, 1965.

Wesley, Charles. *Hymns and Sacred Poems.* New York: Felix Farley, 1749.

Wesley, John. *Journal.* Grand Rapids: Christian Classics Ethereal Library, 1951.

———. *A Plain Account of Christian Perfection.* In Vol. 11, *The Works of John Wesley,* edited by Thomas Jackson, 366–446. Grand Rapids: Zondervan, 1958.

Whittier, John Greenleaf. "Maud Muller." *Poetry Archive.* http://www.poetry-archive.com/w/maud_muller.html.

Williams, Rowan. *Being Disciples:Essentials of the Christian Life.* Grand Rapid: Eerdmans, 2016.

Yancey, Phillip. *The Jesus I Never Knew.* Grand Rapids: Zondervan, 1995.

Young, Carlton R., ed. *The Book of Hymns.* Nashville: Abingdon, 1966.

———. *The United Methodist Hymnal.* Nashville: Abingdon, 1989.

Young, Paul. *The Shack.* Los Angeles: Windblown, 2007.